INNOVATION ON DEMAND

Mary,
Thanks for your
support. See you
at Speaker's network.

Best,
Allen Fahden

Allen Fahden

INNOVATION ON DEMAND

How to benefit from the coming deluge of change: make creativity work for you and your company.

Published by:
The Illiterati
1941 Irving Avenue South
Minneapolis MN 55403

Copyright 1993 by Allen Fahden
First Printing 1991
Second Printing 1993
Printed in the United States of America

Library of Congress Cataloging in Publication Data
Fahden, Allen
Innovation On Demand: How to benefit from the coming deluge of change: make creativity work for you and your company.
/ By Allen Fahden. - 2nd ed.
ISBN 0-9629663-1-2

10   9   8   7   6   5   4   3   2   1

From breakdown to breakthrough.

If you have a breakdown, celebrate.

"Later never exists."
– Author Unknown

To Sybil Lippisch Brown, who taught me about creating.

To Pamela Fahden, who taught me about completing.

"Just remember, we're all in this alone."
  – Lily Tomlin

Many thanks to all the fine people who helped make this book possible.

Sam Namakkal, who pointed the way with inquiry and opportunity.

Thom Sandberg, Ann Riebe, Elizabeth IlgenFritz and John Francis who tried it out in the real world.

Ross Bishop, who spiced up the trip with learning techniques and fun.

Sharon Lavick, Joey Fischman, Louis Hill, David Vergeyle and John Ryan, who advanced the cause with friendship and support.

Debbie Kuehn, Norman Diamond, David Martin, Kris Curoe, Diane Richards, Dave Hakensen and Bill Swanson, who clarified ideas with insight and attention to detail.

Acknowledgments

Joseph Sellars, who beautifully illustrated the cover.

Pamela Fahden, Susan Stuart-Otto, Ron Glodoski, Richard Neuner, Mary McIlrath and Rick LeBurkien, who believed.

Chapter Nine
FOUR STEPS TO OWNING
YOUR CREATIVITY.

Chapter Ten
CREATIVITY ON DEMAND: APPLY
IT ANYWHERE.

Part V
SPECIAL SECTIONS.

Qualitivity
HOW INNOVATION ON DEMAND CAN IMPROVE YOUR PROCESS IMPROVEMENT.

Introduction.
INNOVATION ON DEMAND.

*"He was trying to frame a question
that would take in all the questions
and elicit an answer that would be all
the answers, but it kept coming out so
simple that he distrusted it."*
— Tom Stoppard

This book began in 1977. It was not
important enough to write then. We were
shifting from the "me" decade of the 70's,
(adding the letters "o, n and y") to the
"money" decade of the 80's.

The 80's, with their junk bonds and
leveraged buyouts seemed to be a lot less
about creating, and a lot more about moving
wealth around that already existed. And,
yet, just beneath the obvious, many
profound changes were already setting up
the tumultuous 90's. This book is not so
much about the changes; you need only to
pick up a newspaper to be (sometimes
painfully) aware. Rather, this book is about
how to create the kind of thinking that will

give you power to be the change maker, not
the change casualty.

THERE ARE THOSE WHO MAKE THINGS HAPPEN,
THERE ARE THOSE WHO WATCH THINGS HAPPEN,
AND THERE ARE THOSE WHO WONDER "WHAT HAPPENED?"

Now you have a choice. All you need to
make things happen:

1. Know what you want.
2. Know how to create it.
3. Take action.

This book gives you simple, unique and
powerful ways to get through all three steps.
And once you master all three, you can be a
tremendously effective creator of change.

So if all this is simple, why is it that most
organizations are filled with people who
cannot effectively make change, and many
more who actively resist it? And why does
change cause so much stress?

The truth: nearly everything we are taught
since birth is about keeping things as they
are, rather than changing them.

A recent study tracked Iowa two-year-olds
through one day. It recorded every "no" and
"yes." The score? No: 432; Yes: 14. One
child heard the word "no" so many times he
actually believed it was his name.

Is it any wonder then we are winners at
"no" and losers at "yes?" And when it
comes to making change that early emotions
cloud our thinking and keep us in fear of
thinking, commitment and action?

And, still, today we witness changes that we
would never have thought possible in this
lifetime. The emergence of World War II's
defeated nations, Germany and Japan, as
global economic powers. The tearing down
of the Berlin Wall. The fall of the
Soviet Union.

The question today is, as the CEO of one of
the largest banks in the United States put it:
"Are you on the train? Or under it?"

HOW TWENTY-THREE YEARS OF CREATIVE CHANGE FUELED THE NEW PRINCIPLE OF CREATIVITY.

Most of today's writing on creativity comes out of our schools. Much of the rest comes from consultants.

And yet, creating and implementing change cannot work when left to theory alone, nor can it succeed when a consultant passes out some wisdom and then leaves.

Yes, teachers and consultants begin the process of change in many elegant ways.

Yet, how many programs have died because the people inside the organization couldn't get beyond the roadblocks?

So, here and now, you can experience a step-by-step program of creativity that has made profound organizational change.

One that allowed beginners to out-perform skilled artisans.

One that turned one company's decline into a 150% increase in two years.

Simply by starting with the only agent for effective change: the most basic thinking of the people.

HOW TO CREATE POWERFUL CHANGE: START WITH YOUR THINKING.

Everything starts with our thinking.

How can we change something if we cannot conceive of what we're changing it to?

Nature abhors a vacuum.

THE DIFFERENCE BETWEEN CYCLICAL CHANGE AND STRUCTURAL CHANGE.

So anything we're trying to change away from will keep coming back unless we replace it with something new.

For example: Try not thinking of a horse.
All you'll think about is a horse.

Now, replace the horse with a car. Now
you're not thinking of a horse. How does
this relate to change? First, let's make
a distinction.

As we move into a decade of accelerating
change, we must first be able to distinguish
between the two different types of change:
cyclical and structural.

Cyclical change means literally, changes
that take place in cycles. Example:
Hemlines go up, hemlines go down. Then
they go back up again. Hair gets short, hair
gets long. Then it gets short again. The
Democrats win, the Republicans win. Then
the Democrats win again.

Structural change is dramatically different.
It's that rare moment when something
changes and most likely won't change back.
For example: Mass production: (We have
not returned to the agrarian age.) The
automobile: (We have not returned to

horses and buggies.) The computer: (We have not returned to the slide rule, the typewriter, etc.)

The last of these, the computer, has caused and will continue to cause much of the uncertainty we face today. Example: Mass marketing is dead. It's been replaced by mass customization. Today you can buy a custom-made bicycle for no more than a mass-produced model. For the new thinker this spells opportunity; for the old thinker this spells disaster.

This is the Chinese symbol for crisis. It contains two characters. One of them means opportunity.

BE AN "OPPOTUNITY" THINKER AND NOTHING CAN PASS YOU BY.

As you will see as you read Innovation on Demand, an "Oppotunity" is an opportunity created by a unity of opposites. One might also call this type of thinking contradictory or paradoxical, as well as opposite. The advantage is the same and the need is identical.

In the late 80's and early 90's the United States discovered quality methods that included continuous process improvement. It started in 1947 when W. Edwards Deming was invited to Japan by the Japanese Union of Scientists and Engineers to teach them his methods of continuous process improvement. Not until 1980 did the U.S. discover Deming, long after the Japanese had credited him with their emergence as an economic power.

And Honda marketing people reversed the visual aspect of car design by playing tape recordings of door-slams to consumers. Then they asked their engineers to create a

car with a door-slam that sounds exactly
like the one consumers chose as the highest
quality car. It continued in the U.S. with
Ford, Xerox and other companies turning
quality programs into competitive
advantage. They accomplished this by going
to the opposite of several obvious ways of
doing business.

The lower-downs made the improvements,
not the higher-ups.

Management listened to horizontal (cross-
functional) teams rather than vertical
(specialized) managers or departments.

So, opposites of the obvious are creating
results everywhere in business. And now
you can operate ahead of all but the most
innovative and creative thinkers. The key is
in your hand, so read on.

INNOVATION ON DEMAND

Allen Fahden

Part I
THE FOUR INNOVATION PATTERNS.

Chapter One
IN A PROCESS DRIVEN WORLD, THE INNOVATION PROCESS IS STILL OUT OF CONTROL.

"We are the echo of the future."
   -W. S. Merwin

More and more companies have instituted quality programs that depend on controlling processes. As they get better and better at process, quality will no longer be a basis for competitive advantage, because everyone will have it.

Maybe that's why after winning the 1989 Baldridge Quality Award, Paul Allaire, the CEO of Xerox, said in Fortune Magazine, "We're never going to outdiscipline the Japanese on quality. To win, we need to find ways to capture the creative and innovative spirit of the American worker. That's the real organizational challenge."

The question: How good are companies at innovation? The stories of idea killers and

and cultures that stifle innovation are
legend. To solve this, we first need to
examine why this is so.

PROBLEM #1. Innovation requires
creativity. Without an original and workable
idea, you have little or nothing. The annals
of marketing are filled with companies
that failed because they introduced me-too
products and services. In other words,
without distinction, you're headed
for extinction.

PROBLEM #2. Business has never accepted
creative people. Often, they don't even get
hired. "They're too weird. They won't fit
in." If they do get hired, they get suppressed,
or worse yet, ignored.

PROBLEM #3. Even if they are hired and
valued, creative people suffer under
managers and co-workers who don't
understand how to work with them. One of
the best examples of this can be found in
advertising agencies, where some managers
often secretly describe creative people as a
"necessary evil."

PROBLEM #4. Even when people work together well, they don't always get the best results. That's because people have little or no control over the creative process itself. So, each person works very differently from the next person. In other words, there's still enormous variation left in the creative process. And for those of you who know the methods of quality, the key is to remove variation from processes. This variation leads to trial and error, hit and miss creativity. Worse yet, the culture then leads to people defending their hit and miss work with a ferocity that rivals the worst of wars. That's why much of this book will advance principles and methods that can remove all the trial and error, hit and miss variation from creativity.

THE END OF THE WIPE-OUT OR WIMP-OUT DILEMMA.

Now, back to the corporate culture issue. Most people will either wipe out (create unnecessary conflict) or wimp out (make risky compromises to avoid conflict) when

working with creative people. Either way,
there's a loser. And both ways, anyone who
depends on the quality of the work loses
as well.

In the next chapter you'll share in the
author's more than 20 years of managing
the boundaries between creative people and
their more traditional counterparts. I have
managed these boundaries in my own
award-winning creative "boutique," and as
Creative Director of several advertising
agencies. This experience includes
mediating between both sides so that the
most powerful, effective concepts can live.

In your context this means that no matter
what company you're in, you can work
with creative people and move ahead
through the selling and refining of ideas
to final implementation.

After all, until an idea is actually implemented,
it means nothing.

The next chapter will also explain common
blunders that many managers make with

creative people, and how to adopt new ways that will avoid these errors and lead to the best possible work.

The key to this success is to know basic motivations that drive each party, and to act in ways that give both people what they need.

In summary, you can't get innovation under control until you:

1. Remove enormous amounts of variation from the creative process.
2. Understand and remove corporate cultural bias.
3. Adopt the new models for success.

SOLUTION: A FRAMEWORK ON WHICH TO BUILD AND MANAGE EFFECTIVE INNOVATION TEAMS.

To change how people work together for innovation, we first need a new model to understand it. One that's based on the full dimensions of the people involved.

Many quadrant systems that measure and graph peoples' tendencies already exist. Yet there are two reasons that none of them work elegantly for innovation.

1. Virtually all matrices deal with only one dimension. They deal with behavior, values or thinking. None that we know of combine the basic two dimensions of innovation: thought and behavior. Why both? Because only in innovation does thought carry so much weight (someone thinks of an idea) and does behavior so profoundly affect thought. (Someone implements or kills the idea with their behavior.)

2. Nowhere in business do people operate under so much stress as during the processes of creativity and innovation. It's stressful to create ideas. (See the Panic/ Elation/Panic Cycle, in Chapter five) It's also stressful to judge new ideas. Especially those that catapult us outside our comfort zone, as all breakthroughs first do.

Chapter Two
INNOVATE WITH C.A.R.E.

"Nobody realizes that some people expend tremendous energy merely to be normal"
    -Albert Camus

This is how C.A.R.E. is different.

1. It's based on thinking and behavior.

Thinking: Linear vs. Conceptual.

Linear is step by step and methodical. The process usually goes: 1, 2, 3, 4, 5. *Conceptual* is to leap to the solution, or even change the whole game. The process can often go: 1, 2, 5, 3, 4.

Behavior: Adopting vs. Changing.

Adopting is the person who waits until the situation is stable and safe to choose a behavior. Then, that person will most often move with the crowd rather than against it.

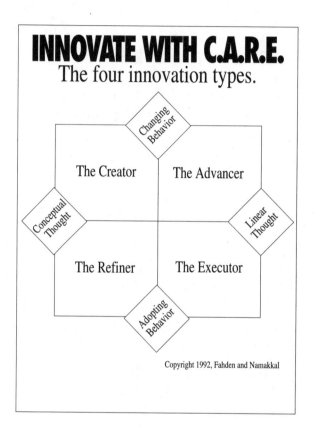

INNOVATE WITH C.A.R.E.
The four innovation types.

Changing Behavior

The Creator

The Advancer

Conceptual Thought

Linear Thought

The Refiner

The Executor

Adopting Behavior

Copyright 1992, Fahden and Namakkal

Changing is the person who chooses to adopt a behavior before it is stable and safe. Then, that person will most often move against the crowd rather than with it.

2. It's based on removing the stress of innovation. C.A.R.E. deals with the boundaries between each group to promote

understanding and cooperation. No group is
of any more or less value than any other.
And in fact, a team that's missing at least
one person from one group is in danger.
And if the team is missing persons from two
groups, it may have some huge struggles.

THE FOUR INNOVATION TYPES, DESCRIBED.

CREATOR. The Creator generates the
concept. When a structure or a rule exists,
the Creator will break it. The Creator
derives satisfaction from the process of
creation, and seeing the idea implemented.
CONTRIBUTION: Fresh, original
concepts. STRENGTHS: Ability to think
outside the normal patterns and paradigms.
WEAKNESSES: If left alone to refine
concepts, the Creator will solve the problem
within the problem, and eventually lose
sight of the objective. BEHAVIOR: Starts
new direction.

ADVANCER. The Advancer moves the
concept forward. When an idea is first

presented, the Advancer immediately thinks about how to get it implemented. The Advancer derives satisfaction from the process of selling the idea and removing all roadblocks to its success.
CONTRIBUTION: Energetic pursuit of implementation. STRENGTHS: Eagerness, support and persistence. WEAKNESSES: If working only with the Creator, the Advancer will often move ahead to implement concepts that aren't completely thought through, setting up later problems. BEHAVIOR: Advances new direction.

REFINER. The Refiner challenges the concept. When a concept is presented, the Refiner will play the "devil's advocate." The Refiner derives satisfaction from the mental exercise of the debate, and causing others to consider options the Refiner has created. CONTRIBUTION: Making sure the concept is thought through. STRENGTHS: Ability to create a potentially valid concept opposite the Creator's. WEAKNESSES: If allowed to dominate the group, the Refiner will either stop the process or lead the team toward a another direction. BEHAVIOR: Vacillates between new and old directions.

EXECUTOR. The Executor carries out the will of the team. Until an idea is ready for implementation, the Executor has little interest. The Executor derives satisfaction from finishing the job with as little upset as possible. CONTRIBUTION: The detailed tasks of implementation. STRENGTHS: Willingness, thoroughness and the ability to bring up executional flaws early enough to solve inexpensively. WEAKNESSES: If working without frequent and specific direction, the Executor can lose sight of concept and pursue other directions. BEHAVIOR: Waits until new direction is established.

There is also a fifth, or "balanced," pattern called the Facilitator. This person helps the other groups work together more smoothly and productively.

HOW THE FOUR INNOVATION PATTERNS WORK MOST EFFECTIVELY TOGETHER.

They work best when everyone is there and everyone is valued. The dangers of missing team members are many. For example, Creators love Advancers. An Advancer will run with the idea and do everything possible to make it a reality. The danger, however, lies in the extreme. If only the Advancer and Creator work together, they could proceed a long way down the wrong path before a Refiner challenged their thinking.

Or if an Advancer and Refiner got together without a Creator, they'd most likely sophisticate a me-too idea, and fail in a marketplace that demands something different.

If the Creator and Refiner got together without the Advancer, the project would probably get hung up in the debate, and nothing much would ever happen.

If any or all of them proceeded without the Executor, they'd most likely put out a product or service without all the necessary details thought out and acted upon.

The point: Every team needs all the patterns to succeed.

And not only must they be present, they must truly collaborate. For example, if an Advancer dominates the team, the same result of a fast-paced, ill-thought-out product or service introduction might follow.

Example: Bill's company had a reputation for getting things done fast, but had no credibility when it came to strategy. After testing for the four C.A.R.E. patterns, he found the company had a large percentage of Advancers and Executors.

This meant the company had few conceptual thinkers, so anything other than the way they had always thought about things caused great discomfort. In their linear thinking, they denied any attempts at innovation, hoping it would go away. And since there were so many Advancers and

Executors, innovation usually did go away.
But Bill was committed to changing the
company to an innovative organization. So,
whenever he hired anyone, he tested them
for their C.A.R.E. pattern and hired Creators
to originate the work and Refiners to check
it. Soon, Bill had balanced out the
organization and made sure each team had
an equal number of patterns. The new
Creators and Refiners soon led the way to a
new kind of thinking, which the Advancers
and Executors then embraced and moved
forward. Today, Bill's company is known as
one of the most strategic and innovative in
its business.

(If you're interested in the C.A.R.E. test and
system, write or call the author in care of
the publisher listed in the front of the book.)

Chapter Three
HOW TO CREATE THE NEW INNOVATION TEAM: HANDLE WITH C.A.R.E.

*"In the highlands of New Guinea,
I saw men with photographs of
themselves mounted on their foreheads,
so they would be recognized"*
-Ted Carpenter

What makes this team different?

1. The people chosen from thinking and behavior models specifically tuned to the needs of the process of innovation.

2. The methods specifically chosen and created for the critical needs of fast-paced innovation teams. They come from the best of marketing, quality, creativity and team-building development.

3. Understanding respectful ways to get the best from the Creator, the innovation pattern that companies have least understood and valued, is the one that will make a critical contribution to avoiding a "me-too" product or service.

THE C.A.R.E. TEAM, STEP-BY-STEP.

Use the flow chart to plan, create and generate your own team. The chart is purposely general for two reasons.

1. So you can own it and build in the details that best suit you.

2. Because everything in it you already know how to do, someone else knows it and can do it, or you'll know how to do it after finishing this book.

Step one: Develop objectives and scope. LEADER: DEPARTMENT HEAD, V.P. or C.E.O. Start with <u>who</u> wants <u>what</u> done by <u>when</u>? If it's a boss or customer, get their expectations and criteria for success down before you start. Get any constraints as well, especially money and time. For criteria, use the issues grid in chapter 19, and find what's important to the internal or external customer you're serving.

Step two: Create team selection criteria.
LEADER: DEPARTMENT HEAD, V.P. or C.E.O. Some example criteria that will help you avoid costly problems later:

1. Teams should be cross-functional so entire scope of project is covered. Ford developed the Taurus with team members from engineering, design, manufacturing, dealer sales, service, vendors and, yes, even customers. Many of these people had never talked to one another.

2. Teams should include all four C.A.R.E. types with Refiners from every functional group. (Give them C.A.R.E. tests.)

Step three: Select team.
LEADER: DEPARTMENT HEAD, V.P. or C.E.O. Choose those that best fit criteria and can make significant commitment to the team.

Step four: Align the team.
LEADER: FACILITATOR.

1. Promote the value and respect for all
C.A.R.E. pattern members. (See C.A.R.E.
pattern explanations.)

2. Teach consensus process: You'll never
get agreement from everyone, therefore
team members need only reach <u>consensus</u>.
Consensus means all members can back
direction <u>without</u> giving up their personal
needs, i.e., "It's not my idea, but I can live
with it."

Step five: Develop strategy.
LEADER: REFINER.

1. Start with the description of your target
market. Research their needs and wants and
how well they're currently being satisfied.
Find out what irritates them about the
present way those needs are being met.

2. Then develop an issues grid (See chapter
19) for the category you're in, i.e., if you're
developing a new camera, do a grid for
photography, then tighten in to cameras.
Why a broader grid first? There may be a
better way than cameras to do photography.

3. Select the important issues everyone needs to improve on. Innovate there, and you have a potential market leader. Do it at the lowest cost and you'll keep your lead.

Step six: Create concept.
LEADER: CREATOR. Use obvious opposites to create the most innovative concepts. (See chapters 8-14.) Go for a product or service advantage first. If you don't have a significant advantage there, next try for a service delivery advantage. Failing that, go for a creative advantage.

EXAMPLES:
Product advantage: A car with ABS brakes. Service delivery advantage: A car with free oil changes for life.
Creative advantage: A car with colors that match your eyes and skin.

Step seven: Test concept.
LEADER: ADVANCER. Once you have the best idea, test it against your second , third and fourth best options. Go back to similar people in the market who told you their issues and have them rate how your new

idea performs in direct contrast to the
products and services they rated before.
Once that test is successful, try it inside
with people you trust not to kill or
undermine it. Find out: "Can we make it?"
"Can we deliver on this promise?" "Does
this fit the company's mission, vision and
strategy?" If not, revise.

Step eight: Plan implementation.
LEADER: REFINER. Write a business plan
for your idea.

1. Show everything from steps five through
seven; that's your opportunity.

2. Show potential share of market,
investment needed and payback. The best
innovations can be paid for out of expenses
they eliminate or by immediate revenues.
People will still spend money to make
more money.

Step nine: Implement.
LEADER: EXECUTOR. Once you have your
plan, approvals and funding, give your
Executors clear direction. Then have your

Advancers manage the schedule. Ask the
Executors to point out any problems to the
Creators. Ask the Creators to give solutions
to Advancers to show to Refiners. Ask the
Creators to solve the Refiners' objections to
their solutions. Then re-direct the Executor
until the next problem comes up. Then
repeat.

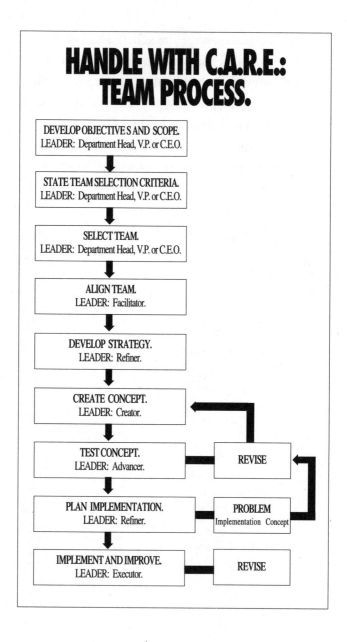

HANDLE WITH C.A.R.E.: TEAM PROCESS.

DEVELOP OBJECTIVES AND SCOPE.
LEADER: Department Head, V.P. or C.E.O.

STATE TEAM SELECTION CRITERIA.
LEADER: Department Head, V.P. or C.E.O.

SELECT TEAM.
LEADER: Department Head, V.P. or C.E.O.

ALIGN TEAM.
LEADER: Facilitator.

DEVELOP STRATEGY.
LEADER: Refiner.

CREATE CONCEPT.
LEADER: Creator.

TEST CONCEPT.
LEADER: Advancer.

REVISE

PLAN IMPLEMENTATION.
LEADER: Refiner.

PROBLEM
Implementation Concept

IMPLEMENT AND IMPROVE.
LEADER: Executor.

REVISE

Part II
UNDERSTANDING CREATORS AND CREATIVITY.

Chapter Four
HOW TO GET THE BEST FROM CREATORS WITHOUT WIPING OUT OR WIMPING OUT.

"Be obscure clearly"
-E. B. White

Now that you know the four innovation types, let's deal with the most difficult one to understand and work with for the mainstream corporation.

To be effective with Creators, we must first know what's important to them. In a word: Recognition.

Creators need to be recognized for their ideas. This need is so strong, one could almost relate it to their survival all the way to their self-realization needs.

Using Maslow's Hierarchy of needs, a conversation with a Creator might look like this on each of Maslow five levels:

Survival: "If I do bad creative work,
I'll die."

Safety: "If I do bad creative work, I'll
die later."

Esteem from others: "Oh, you've seen
my work."

Esteem from self: "Oh, you've seen my
work in the awards shows."

Self-realization: "If I die, I won't care if I
do bad creative work."

If you're going to get the best from
someone, use an opposite. (See Chapter 8)
Give the best to someone. What's important
to creators is the following:

Recognition. They want to be
acknowledged for their brilliance. But,
beware. Ernest Hemingway said that "every
good writer has a built-in crap detector."
And so does every Creator. So, when you
praise, be authentic.

Authenticity. A Creator will believe you're authentic in your praise when you truly understand the idea. A Creator will believe you truly understand the idea when you've asked enough questions and fed back enough of your understanding so you both get that you understand the idea.

Questions. A Creator is not always interested in your opinions. In fact, many times your negative opinion can appear as a threat to the idea. Therefore, you can accomplish the same end by questioning. If your opinion is that the idea is too dangerous, ask: "What possible dangers do you see if we go with this idea?" The answers will put both of you in a Refiner's role, contributing greatly to lack of surprise or blunder down the road.

Distinctiveness. Creators also love to be different. In fact, many Creators have to be different. It's like when Author Stephen King was asked why he wrote all those bizarre horror stories, he allegedly replied, "You don't think I have any choice, do you?"

If the idea is different, acknowledge *how* it's different. **Example:** Compare it to the present way of doing things and show how the new idea stands out in a positive way: "I see. Instead of waiting for a receipt, the customer could choose at the beginning not to get one." Then acknowledge the *advantage* of doing it differently: "That's why the idea would save time." Then get feedback on whether you got it: "Do I understand the idea?"

Importance. If the idea is important, acknowledge *how* it's important. **Example:** Put the idea into a broader context that makes it important: "Well, this is the 90's, and in the 90's people certainly need to save every minute of time they can get. This is a powerful idea because time-saving innovations are very successful lately." Then give an example of how that's true.

Breaking rules. Creators love to break the rules, so acknowledge how they did it in a *constructive* way. That gives them the satisfaction of getting away with something in a *legal* way, so they won't have to pay a price. That's one part that makes business fun for a Creator. In school they couldn't break the rules. If they did, they would often end up being wrong or bad because the system needed them to conform. The same has been true in corporations. If they broke the rules there, they would be considered "not part of the team" and place their careers in jeopardy. Well, now we're moving towards a *new* system. One that's beginning to value innovation above conformity.

HOW YOU REFINERS CAN GET WHAT YOU WANT BY GIVING CREATORS WHAT THEY WANT.

Let's say you're a Refiner. When the Creator gives you output you need:

Meaningful options. More than one idea, so you can discuss, evaluate and, together, choose.

Executable concepts. An idea that you can't roll out is not a viable idea.

Best solution. The Creator should tell you
which solution she deems best and why.
This will give you better evaluating
perspective.

When the Refiner gives the Creator
feedback, the Creator wants:

Big picture. The Creator needs the entire
context from which you're evaluating the
idea. **Example:** You're thinking of the
European market, too, and the idea doesn't
translate well.

Full disclosure. Hold back no information
that can contribute to the best solution,
especially problems caused by the idea.
You'll only end up with an idea that doesn't
completely work for you. **Example:** If you
hate red, just say that it's not a bad idea, but
you just have a personal problem with red.
If red isn't important to the success of the
idea, the Creator may be willing to make
it green.

Problems, not solutions. Don't solve the
problem for the Creator, then give him the

solution. That's the Creator's job. You'll
only get resistance. Instead, present your
problem with his solution so he can solve it.
Strategy, not just data. Think about the
information you provide for the Creator. If
you give her reams of data to plow through,
you're not using her well. Instead, get the
whole team to go through the data and
decide what it means first. Filter the
unimportant data first. (See Issues Grid,
chapter 19) Add some history of what *didn't*
work before and why.

Then you'll send the Creator to work with
specific clear direction.

Chapter Five
THE PARADOX: WITHOUT A RELIABLE METHOD, THE VERY THOUGHT OF HAVING TO CREATE CAUSES ENOUGH FEAR AND ANXIETY TO SHUT DOWN YOUR CREATIVITY.

"Is it on?"
> – Three-year-old boy holding
> ball-point pen.

In hundreds of creativity trainings, people have routinely reported emotions like fear, anger, anxiety, frustration and physical symptoms such as shortness of breath, tightness in the chest and an overall feeling of panic.

Why should this be? Isn't creating supposed to be childlike and fun? It is until someone tells you to be childlike and have fun.

Here's what actually happens.

1. The creative process normally starts with panic, accompanied by thoughts like, "I'll never have a good idea." (The exception is those who are used to creating. Then, the first thought is usually something like: "I'm glad they called on me to do this" with a feeling of pride, which then turns into panic.)

2. With the first idea, the panic turns to elation. "What a great idea. I could be famous."

3. Then comes the thought: "How will others react to my idea? Maybe they'll think I'm stupid," which then leads to panic and fear all over again.

THE P.E.P. CYCLE.

"What a good idea."

"I'll never have a good idea."

"I'll really look stupid with this idea."

PANIC   ELATION   PANIC

WE PUT PEOPLE ON THE MOON, YET WE HAVEN'T MASTERED CREATIVITY.

Just as it's exciting to play games of chance, it's exciting to create. The underlying fear of loss can make an exciting game, but the loss itself can cause shame or lower self-esteem. Think of the last time you lost at any gambling game, and then think of the conversation you had with yourself. It was most likely not uplifting.

THE FEAR PARADOX: MOST CREATIVE METHODS CAUSE ANXIETY.

Until now, people have approached creativity with methods that try to cover nearly every contingency. "Try this, it'll make you more creative." "Try this, it'll make you more playful." "Try meditation." "Try observing nature."

These methods can be very powerful and productive. Yet they can also wind up in dead ends, wasted time and discourage the user.

In fact, studies have shown that excessive choice causes anxiety. So, too many choices of creative methods could cause enough anxiety to shut down the creativity you're trying to access.

THE IRONY: IN A FIELD AS "CREATIVE" AS CREATIVITY, THERE HAS BEEN LITTLE INNOVATION.

After the Father of Brainstorming, Alex Osborne, developed his landmark book, *Applied Imagination* in 1948, there has been little new in the area of creativity. Even though Synectics taught us that instead of creating from nothing, we combine. And although Edward DeBono has made significant advances with Lateral Thinking, most of the advances have missed the core issue: There is a single attribute present in all powerfully new ideas.

SO MANY METHODS, SO LITTLE DIRECT POWER.

What's more, when faced with so many methods to try, you're much more likely to choose methods that don't work. Rather than help you solve the problem every time, most approaches have simply given you a little of this and a little of that without giving you the direct route to a reliable solution.

This can often discourage the person using the method. "If this doesn't work for me, it must be because I can't do it. I knew I wasn't creative."

Rather, the truth is there have been no theoretical advancements in creativity in the last 20 to 30 years. And yet the need for creativity and innovation in business is getting greater and greater.

THE CREATIVITY PRINCIPLE: HOW IT'S DIFFERENT.

Once you finish this chapter, you'll never again have to endure the anxiety of chance in creativity. Rather, you can approach each problem with the confidence you truly have a place to start that's going to lead you directly to a powerful solution.

That's because the simple, quick creativity method you're going to learn is based on something that other methods, useful as they are, have missed: the single principle that's present in all powerful ideas, and missing from those ideas that are ordinary.

MYTH #1: ONLY A BLESSED FEW HAVE THE GIFT OF CREATIVITY.

Not so. Rather, you all have the gift. You've just been talked out of using it. And to make matters worse, you most likely don't remember when or how. So until now, you've been helpless to correct it.

MYTH #2: CREATIVITY CANNOT BE TAUGHT.

The reason that people believe creativity can't be taught is that it has not been taught successfully. To assume, therefore, that it cannot be taught is much like assuming the Wright Bothers would never have gotten off the ground. Just because one hasn't seen it happen doesn't mean it cannot happen.

MYTH #3: CREATIVITY IS A MYSTICAL ACT.

Creativity is a process, just like washing the dishes or starting a car. Unfortunately, no one has made it accessible enough to be understood in a simple way. Once you understand and act on it a few times, it will be as easy as starting your car.

"THE OPPOSITE OF A TRUTH IS NOT NECESSARILY A FALSEHOOD. IT IS OFTEN AN EVEN GREATER TRUTH."

-Neils Bohr
> *Nobel Prize-Winning*
> *Physicist*

This is the secret of all powerful creation. Black is blackest in a field of white. Height is only measured in relation to the ground. If you want to make a murder scene more grisly than ever, play it to happy music.

So the key to powerful creativity: Don't work on the content. Work on the context. If you want black to be its blackest, be sure its context is as white as it can possibly be.

WHY ARE THESE OPPOSITES SO POWERFUL?

They're powerful for the same reason a professional fighter can most likely knock you out and I can't. He and I may both weigh the same, but he hits much harder. Simple physics explains this best.

Force (how hard he hits you) equals Mass (how much he weighs) times Acceleration (how fast he hits you.) Because he can do things with his body that I cannot do with mine, he can accelerate his equal mass into more force than I can.

But don't despair. All is not lost. Try this creative approach to boxing, and you'll see why you don't need to be a pro boxer to create power in all areas of your life.

If you're right-handed, put your right fist one inch from the palm of your open left hand.

Now hit your left hand with your right fist as hard as you can.

What happened? How hard were you able to hit your left hand? Probably not very hard. Most of us don't have the reflexes, speed and strength to create much impact from that close-up.

Now do the same thing again. Only this time, have your right fist one foot away from your left palm. Now hit it again.

Chances are, that hit a lot harder. Why? Simply because you increased the <u>distance</u> over which your fist was traveling, without increasing the <u>time</u>.

This key distinction will allow you to generate powerful concepts and solve nearly impossible problems.

In football, it's why kickers can kick the ball much farther on a kickoff than they can on a field goal attempt. They get a running start. They cover more distance before they reach the ball without adding much time, so

they can generate more acceleration and,
therefore, more force.

That's why if you want to create powerful
concepts, you must create as much distance
as possible between what is and what can
be.

This, then, sets up the running start that
allows you to generate the acceleration.
This, in turn, creates the force that's present
in all powerful ideas.

Now that you have experienced the power
of distance, what is the farthest distance?

The opposite. The universe is made up of
polar opposites. For example: Light/dark. If
you want to have an extreme physical
effect, shift a room from light to dark or
dark to light. Then notice how long it takes
for all the eye muscles in the room
to adapt.

Black/White. If you want to cause stress
enough to create optical illusions, juxtapose
the two opposites, black and white. Gaze

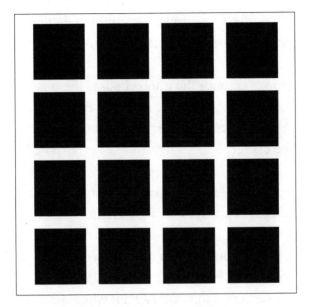

indirectly at the picture. See the gray
squares? They're not there.

WHERE TO FIND THE MOST
POWERFUL OPPOSITES.

From the earliest age we are taught things
about our reality that force us to choose our
behavior. For example, we choose not to
cross busy streets without looking. And we
choose not to put our hands in hot flames.

It's perfectly natural and helpful to do this, because it helps us survive in this world.

However, once the mind chooses these new realities, it holds on to them for dear life. And then we even forget we ever made the choice.

For example, one of the first things we ever learn about stoves is: they are hot.

Imagine yourself as a curious two-year-old who sees a bright blue and orange light flickering on top of this giant white mass in the kitchen. (Or avocado mass. Or harvest gold mass.) As you reach out to experience this wonder with your sense of touch, your peaceful world is suddenly shattered. You see your mother running at you, screaming these sounds over and over again. Later you learn that these sounds are the words, "STOVE! HOT!" and, of course, your mother was terrified that you would be burned.

You forgot only one part. How huge of an imprint this experience might have made on you. After all, if your mother was over five feet tall, and if you at age two were less than three feet tall, in today's scale it would be like having a 10-foot tall giant running at you screaming "STOVE! HOT!" This wouldn't have an impact?

At the time your mother most likely thought "STOVE! HOT!" was very useful information. Because it kept you from getting burned.

It also cemented this association in your mind so you can call on it whenever you want to keep from getting burned.

Unfortunately, the mind also set up another dynamic at the same time. It actually forced you to make a choice you didn't know you were making.

Because the universe is made up of polar opposites, by choosing "STOVE! HOT!" you actually closed off the possibilities of "STOVE! COLD!"

And the truth is, 95% of the time stoves are cold. (The joke in our house is that it's 100% of the time.)

Think about "STOVE! COLD!" Because stoves are metal and metal is a thermal conductor, stoves will tend to be at room temperature when they're not in use. Let's say that room temperature runs about 70 degrees Fahrenheit. Then, let's say normal body temperature runs about 98.6 degrees. That would mean that the stove is 28.6 degrees colder than you are. If you don't think that's "STOVE! COLD!", try getting into a tub of room-temperature bath water. It may not shock you at first, because you're used to touching room temperature objects. But stay in the water for a while and see how cold it really is.

"THE INVISIBILITY OF THE FAMILIAR."

- James Fixx, *Games for the Super Intelligent.*

When things become familiar to us, we tend to forget they even exist.

When we lose sight of certain thoughts and
ideas as habit, we ignore their counterpart or
complement. This causes sights like the
weight lifter who has the perfect upper body
and the thinnest legs you've ever seen. So
what does he do for his workout? You
guessed it. He stares intently in the mirror
while he does nothing but upper body
exercises, ignoring his legs and getting his
body farther and farther out of balance.

HAVE A COMFORTABLE LEARNING EXPERIENCE.

Psychologists tell us certain body positions
are not only comfortable, but also
emotionally comforting. To make this point,
try the following: Sit back, cross your legs
at the ankles and slump in your chair. Then,
lace your fingers across your stomach. Now
just let every muscle relax. Take a couple of
deep breaths. Pretty relaxing, isn't it?

Now, try this. Lace your fingers the
opposite way. In other words, put the
fingers of one hand into the grooves on the

other side of the fingers of the other hand.
Now, observe what happens to your
relaxation. Notice the muscles in your arms,
your back, your neck. Do they tense up?
Notice what just happened to your
breathing. If you're like most people, not
only did your muscles tighten up, and your
breathing get shallow, but some kind of
internal alarm could have even gone off,
beeping and screaming "damage control,
damage control!"

And you made that huge leap from comfort
to discomfort simply by changing only the
position of your fingers.

WHEN DID YOU DECIDE HOW TO LACE YOUR FINGERS?

Probably earlier than you remember. The
point is that you did decide, and then you
forgot you decided. How many other
decisions about reality did you make in
exactly the same way? For most of us,
thousands. And that's where many of our
opportunities lie. Because, buried right

under your nose, and just past your habits,
are powerful ideas.

Now you may have always thought those
powerful ideas were so hard to conceive.
Not so. They're right in front of you. If you
can only see them.

WHY IS THIS METHOD SO POWERFUL AND USEFUL? LET'S APPLY "INNOVATION ON DEMAND" TO THE AREA OF CREATIVITY.

THE OBVIOUS: most creativity methods are
indirect. They tend to deal with the
environment for creating ideas rather than
the core principle.

THE OPPOSITE: a direct creativity method
based on the core principle.

THE OBVIOUS: most creativity methods are
multi-faceted. They tend to give you many
ways to get to the answer.

THE OPPOSITE: a singular creativity method
where you need to learn only one thing to
get it to work for you.

THE OBVIOUS: with most creativity methods you must go outside your comfort zone to some mystical, unknown place.

THE OPPOSITE: a creativity method that keeps you inside your comfort zone at all times, because you know exactly where you're going. (To the opposite.)

THE OBVIOUS: most creativity methods are slow.

THE OPPOSITE: a fast creativity method.

THE OBVIOUS: most creativity methods are based on mastering something outside yourself. (Analogies from nature, for example.)

THE OPPOSITE: a creativity method that's based on mastering something inside yourself. (Seeing past your blind spots to the obstinate obvious.)

THE TOUGHER THE PROBLEM, THE MORE POWERFUL THE SOLUTION.

Now that you've had some experience with the Innovation on Demand principle, use your new-found creativity to improve your life.

Write down your toughest problem, and label it "The obvious." Then write "The opposite" and state the opposite of your problem. Then ask, "how could this opposite be true?"

Example: The Obvious: I have a big nose.

The Opposite: I have a small nose. How true? I have a small nose and an even smaller face. If I hold my jaw out a little more, my nose will look smaller by comparison.

SET SOME GROUND RULES FOR YOUR MIND.

Once you discover this new idea, your mind is going to want to reject it (based on all

your past habits and internal
"conversations" with yourself.) Don't let
that happen or you are right back where
you started.

Instead, adopt some ground rules for your
creativity sessions, similar to the kind the
professionals use for brainstorming
sessions. Nothing kills an idea faster than
your internal voice, offering judgments to
"protect you from looking stupid with a bad
idea." Unfortunately, anything that hasn't
already been done before safely looks like a
bad idea to that judgment machine
(your mind.)

Therefore, get control of your mind by
adopting and sticking to these ground rules
in all your idea generation sessions.

FORNESS. Focus your thoughts on the ways
you are *for* an idea. There are no bad ideas.
Some are just more elegant than others.

MORENESS. Focus your thoughts on the
ways you can *add* to an idea once you have

it, and the ways which you keep the process
moving forward towards what you want.
Beware of detours.

EXPLORENESS. Focus your thoughts on the
fact that you are now *exploring* the other
half of reality, the one you have been
covering with your blind spots, so all these
new ideas might not fit your current
opinions. This may be the best reason to
adopt them, and get yourself unblinded
and unstuck.

GALORENESS. Focus your thoughts on the
fact you will never run out of ideas because
there are so *many* blind spots to explore.
Keep going until you've contributed real
value to your situation.

SOARNESS. Focus your thoughts on the
fact that a new idea is indeed a fragile thing,
one that can be battered by the judgments
and opinions of others. Seize the moment
just before your first fear of judgment, when
the idea was fresh and joyful. Prolong this
moment and *soar* with it.

Follow these ground rules and use your newfound creativity process to move towards your dreams.

SATISFACTION WITHOUT ACTION IS REDUCED TO SATISF.

The world is full of "woulda, coulda, shoulda" stories. They're all based on ideas that someone didn't act on. What do you want? Another story? Or a life that works the way you've always wanted it to?

So, once you choose your most promising idea, get moving. And don't worry if the path looks long and tiring. If you're truly inspired by the idea of finally getting what you want, you'll stay with it. But you must re-inspire yourself every moment. Recommit to what you want every morning, and give it some time every day. And do it before all of your obligations push it out of your life, and back into a "woulda, coulda, shoulda."

"HOW DO YOU EAT AN ELEPHANT? ONE BITE AT A TIME."

-Anon.

Start now to implement your idea. Do at
least one action per day for a week to move
that idea forward. Don't fall into the trap
that you have to do it all now. A lot of
people will get inspired and think they can
do it all at once. But this is just flying from
one extreme to another. And because of
Newton's first Law of Motion (for every
action, there is an equal and opposite
reaction) you may be setting yourself up for
failure by trying to do it all at once and then
giving up.

HOW TO SUCCEED: FAIL FASTER.

By committing to one smaller action per
day, you can do, fail and learn in small bits
that will eventually get you through the
maze to exactly where you want to be.
Pilots do this all the time (or in many planes

now, their computers do it.) It's called
navigation, and simply put, it goes like this:

1. Set a course.
2. Go.
3. See what's happening with the wind.
4. Repeat.

Then at the end of the first week, look back
and see how far it's gotten you. You'll be
pleasantly surprised how much you can
accomplish by keeping your dreams in
balance with the rest of your life. Do the
same for the next week. And the next.

Chapter Six
THE PROBLEM: BLIND SPOTS.

*"What we remember can be changed.
What we forget we are always."*
– Richard Shelton

If experience were truly the best teacher,
few things would ever go wrong. But thanks
to our blind spots, it's more like this quote.

"BEWARE THE CRAFTSMAN WHO CLAIMS TWENTY YEARS OF EXPERIENCE. IT'S OFTEN JUST ONE YEAR OF EXPERIENCE OVER AND OVER AGAIN TWENTY TIMES."

-Anon

So if experience alone doesn't create the
results you need, then what does? You'll
find the answer on a slightly higher level.
On the level of laws and principles. You can
be doing creative work for 20 years and
having exactly the same problems now as
when you started.

That's because you've had no operating
principle that would get you out of the
problems.

WE LOSE 90% OF OUR CREATIVITY BETWEEN THE AGES OF 5 AND 7.

What happens between five and seven to sap our creative juices? Simple: We go to school. We learn to color between the lines. We learn to follow the rules. We learn to make judgments: There is a right and wrong way to do something. In short, we conform.

Our minds learn, in those early years, to embrace and cling to certain parts of reality. We shut down the other parts. The result is we form some bizarre conclusions.

BLIND SPOTS ARE AS OLD AS WISDOM ITSELF.

"Speaking movies are impossible...It will never be possible to synchronize the voice with the picture." So said the famous filmmaker, D.W. Griffith, in the early 1920s. "The Grand Canyon is, of course, altogether valueless. Ours has been the first, and will doubtless be the last, party of whites to visit this profitless locality." So wrote Lt. Joseph C. Ives of the Army Corps of Topographical Engineers in 1861.

In 1903 the U.S. Congress passed a special bill forbidding the Army to waste any more money on trying out flying machines. At the same time the patent office was refusing applications for such machines. In December of that year, the Wright brothers flew their airplane at Kitty Hawk.

"I tell you," said Napoleon to his generals over breakfast, "Wellington is a bad general; the English are bad soldiers. We will settle this matter before lunch."

"Everything that can be invented has been invented."
> - Charles H. Duell, Director of the
> U.S. Patent Office, 1899.

"Who the hell wants to hear actors talk?'
> - Harry Warner, Warner Bros.
> Pictures, 1927.

TEST FOR YOUR OWN BLIND SPOT.

X   ●

      Hold the paper 6-8 inches from your face, cover your left eye and stare at the X with your right eye. As you move the paper in and out slowly, the dot should disappear from your peripheral vision.

      This lets you experience your physical blind spot, the place where your optic nerve connects to the retina.

      Think of it as a reminder of all the other perceptual blind spots.

"Sensible and responsible women do not
want to vote."
> - Grover Cleveland, 1905.

"There is no likelihood man can ever tap
the atom."
> - Robert Millikan, Nobel Prize
>   in Physics, 1920.

"Ruth made a big mistake when he gave up
pitching."
> - Tris Speaker, 1921.
>   (From a TRW ad, 1985.)

PERCEPTION IS REALITY.

The truth is that facts change. Consider a so
called business fact: "The Japanese started
manufacturing quality products that
saturated the U.S. market in the early
1980's." Actually, the Japanese surpassed us
in producing quality goods in 1968, but we
didn't catch on to it until the early '80's.
Why didn't we catch on earlier? Because a
new idea, like people flying, needs
popularity in order to be accepted. The more

people "believe" in an idea —accepting it as a possibility—the more it becomes a "fact," which is the opposite of the previously held "fact."

HOW TO SURVIVE LONG ENOUGH TO THRIVE.

Seven out of 10 new businesses fail in the first year. And nine of 10 new products die in about the same period of time, almost always because they fail to get above the noise, the most intense communications clutter in history.

For example, pick out a place where there's a lot of background noise. Speak to someone in a normal voice. See what happens. If they can't hear you, they may ignore you or ask you to speak up. If they ask you to speak up, speak in the same normal voice level. Then see what happens. Eventually, they'll stop trying to hear you and start ignoring you. (If they're polite, they might even say "I'm sorry, I can't hear you," and then ignore you.)

IF YOUR BUSINESS DOESN'T GET ABOVE THE NOISE LEVEL, YOU'RE FINISHED ALMOST AS SOON AS YOU START.

Imagine how easy it is for your business to fail to get above the noise.

The average vocabulary has 8,000 words. The average supermarket has 12,000 brands.

Is it any wonder, then, that businesses have a problem getting even the most basic awareness? There is just no place in the human mind to put all the information we are bombarded with.

Think of the mind as a filing cabinet.

When you see something new, your experience is much like processing your mail in your own office. First, you evaluate what the new information is; then you try to figure out what to do with it. Most new information gets thrown away at this point. "It's not worth keeping," you conclude, and out it goes, never to be remembered again.

If you decide to keep it, you then look for a place to file it, so you can find it again when you need it.

On a few rare occasions, something is encountered again and again, so you finally do make a folder for it. But in a world where the amount of information doubles every 20 months, your chance of being encountered again and again by the mind grows smaller and smaller.

"Everyone is famous for 15 minutes."
      -Andy Warhol

Out of 1,500 to 1,800 messages a day, many of them about these new businesses and products, you'd be hard-pressed to recall even five. Go ahead, try it. Identify five advertisements you've seen or heard in the last 24 hours. OK. How about four? Three? Can you remember even one?

The point is that everyone is trying to do what you're doing, so the noise level is

incredible. Which means, to succeed, you
need a strategy that can get you above
the din.

Chapter Seven
THE PROBLEM WITH PROBLEM SOLVING.

"I don't paint things. I only paint the difference between things."
– Henri Matisse

In a workshop, I heard the idea of content and context explained more elegantly and simply than ever before.

Imagine a bowl of fruit. If you have a problem with the bowl of fruit and you think like most people, that's where you'll look to solve the problem. And if you're like most people, you won't solve it. Or if you do solve it, you won't remove the cause, so the problem with the fruit will return.

So how do you solve a problem powerfully? Think of the fruit as the content, and the bowl as the context.

If you work on the content (the fruit), you'll just be replacing bruised bananas. But if you work on the context (the bowl,) you can find the cause of the problem and remove it. (Maybe the bowl has sharp edges that bruise the bananas so you can place the bananas more carefully, or you'll get a different bowl.) Key principle: when you want to solve a problem, solve it on a higher level. Or put another way, pay attention to the bowl, and you'll have better fruit.

ARISTOTLE SAID IT BEST.

Aristotle, in his Nichomachean Ethics, showed how you can always solve a problem by elevating it to a higher level. In other words, moving from the fruit to the bowl; moving from facts to principles.

Let's say that you operate on facts and are proud of it. Great.

Fact: When faced with danger, man automatically gets into a "flight or fight" mode. So, if you look at this from a fact level, these are your only two options.

However, if you move up to the principle level, you'll see that the opposites of flight and fight are simply one side of a larger coin (on the principle level.) Flight and fight make up the side of resistance. Yet on the other side of that coin is the principle of acceptance. And if you choose acceptance, your power increases dynamically. You don't have to fight or run.

For example, new technology now allows you to shoot photos directly onto a computer disk, therefore quickly bypassing film and processing.

If you make or process film, you can resist and slowly go out of business. Or, accept and find a way to co-exist with the new technology and even benefit from it.

One opportunity is to say, "slow is good," a great opposite from today's speed-sensitive culture. How is slow good? It's the only way you can get the so-called "film look" which can now represent the high quality, high craftsmanship path. The segment may be small, but maybe now you can get a premium price for it.

BEING AGAINST SOMETHING CREATES IT.

There's yet another reason to move from resistance to acceptance. You may have heard the old saying, "what we resist persists." Arnold Patent, author of *You Can Have It All*, has suggested in a workshop that people who are against something actually create the energy for those who are for it. Pro-Life people create Pro-Choice people and vice versa.

JUST WHAT ARE WE PROTECTING OURSELVES FROM?

Most of us don't know. We just get a feeling ranging from vague unease all the way up to panic when one of these opposing ideas presents itself.

Ironically, these very ways of protecting ourselves are what keep us from getting fulfilled. So we are literally protecting ourselves from success.

THERE'S NOTHING AS SCARY AS LETTING GO.

When tiny children are frightened, they do one thing. They hang on. Tight.

Isn't it nice to know that after all these years, nothing has changed?

When mature adults get frightened, they hang on tight. To habits, beliefs, facts and defenses.

What are you hanging on to? A business approach that doesn't work?

A bad investment you think could maybe turn around?

Until you can let go of the habit that doesn't work, there's no room for the behavior that does work.

We live in a universe of polar opposites. What's more, the opposites balance each other out. Good balances evil. Light balances dark. Black balances white.

The universe must maintain its balance, so
if we allow things to go too far to one side,
like a pendulum, they will come swinging
back. Or consider radio comedian Fibber
McGee's closet from the 1940's radio
program. McGee would stuff so much junk
into his closet, that sooner or later when he
opened the door, it would all come tumbling
down on top of him in a loud crash.

This can be true with everything else in life.
If we lean too far to the left or right, the
energy starts to build up in the vacuum
we've created on the other side. If we
continue to ignore it, the vacuum gets
stronger, the noise louder and louder. If we
still ignore it, finally it will get our attention
with a big burst.

THE CHINESE WORD FOR "CRISIS" HAS TWO CHARACTERS. ONE OF THEM MEANS OPPORTUNITY.

The Chinese understand the need for
balance and structure of the universe unlike
many Western countries.

Even the Chinese ways of representing the
universal opposites, Yin and Yang, show us
a reality we don't expect. For in the large
field of white, you'll find a small black dot.
And in the large field of black, you'll find a
small white dot.

In other words, no matter which side of the
pole you're on, you'll always find the seed
of its own opposite contained within. So, if
you're unhappy that current style dictates
hair is short, don't worry: long hair is
coming soon. And there's already a small
group of people who already want long hair
as represented by the small dot.

This small dot is also good news for you,
because your newfound creativity starts
here.

WHY DO WE NEED TO SOLVE PROBLEMS?

It seems like an obvious answer. But as you'll see throughout the book, it's the obstinate obvious that keeps us stuck in many of our problems.

Webster defines PROBLEM as "a situation that presents difficulty, uncertainty or perplexity."

Many of us seek to remove these situations from our lives and work. In fact, many days, that's just about all we do. So why not be as good at problem-solving as you possibly can? It may not give you a life completely free of "difficulty, uncertainty or perplexity," but you can be a lot more comfortable than you are now.

THE NORMAL PROBLEM SOLVING PROCESS. IT USUALLY CREATES MORE PROBLEMS.

First, let's look at what usually goes on when someone attempts to solve a problem.

Step One: "I have a problem." (I'm feeling some discomfort.)

Step Two: "This is the problem." (Things aren't the way I expect them to be.)

Step Three: "Here are some possible solutions." (This should get things back to the way I want them to be.)

Step Four: "This is the best solution." (This looks like it will fix things without causing me any more discomfort.)

Step Five: "I'll try this one." (Take action.) If it works, the problem solver is back in a state of comfort, until the next problem comes up.

If it doesn't work, the problem solver stays in discomfort.

THE INVISIBLE MADE VISIBLE.

What really goes on looks more like this:

The person in discomfort is really in the problem stage for only the first two steps of the process.

Step One: "I have a problem." (I'm feeling some discomfort.)

Step Two: "This is the problem." (Things aren't the way I expect them to be.)

The minute you list some possible solutions, you enter the opportunity stage of the process. After all, if things were to change to any of the solutions, this would mean they would probably be better (causing less discomfort) than in either steps one or two.

Webster defines an opportunity as "a favorable or advantageous combination of circumstances."

So by accomplishing
Step Three: "Here are some possible solutions." (This should get things back to the way I want them to be.)

And Step Four: "This is the best solution."
(This looks like it will fix things without
causing me any more discomfort,) you
clearly focus on the opportunity at hand.

This, unfortunately, is also where many of
us set ourselves up for disappointment.
Because, after **Step Five:** "I'll try this one,"
(Take action) comes a hidden set of steps
which almost always come as either a
surprise or a solution killer.

THE HIDDEN STEPS.

Any time you take action, you're bound to
encounter resistance somewhere.

This emerges in the form of a BARRIER.

Webster defines a barrier as "anything that
impedes or prevents entry or passage."

Think of it as the new problem created by
your solution to your first problem. So, you
have a problem; you think of an opportunity

to solve it, then your opportunity creates another problem.

This is where many people give up. "I didn't think it would be so hard," says the discouraged problem-solver.

It's not so hard. All you need to do is see problems as they really are and add a few simple steps.

Most people give up because the barrier to their solution plunges them right back into discomfort and pain. Why does this happen again and again?

Larry Wilson, best-selling co-author of *The One-Minute Sales Person* and author of *Changing the Game*, has a revealing definition:

"PAIN: The difference between how we expect things to be and how they really are."

We expect that once we apply a solution, the problem will go away. Yet, most of the time, almost the opposite happens. Not only does the original problem stay, but the BARRIER (the problem with your solution) also appears.

How to win? Add Steps Six and Seven.

Step Six: "Here are some possible solutions to the barrier." (When I get past my disappointment, this problem isn't so hard.)

Step Seven: "This is the best solution." (I'll make sure the original problem still gets solved.)

Step Eight: Repeat Step Five "I'll try this one." (Take action.) and continue through Step Eight until you're out of discomfort.

HOW PROBLEMS, OPPORTUNITIES AND BARRIERS HELP TURN AROUND A FAILING COMPANY.

Don saw a great opportunity in a failing company. No one had been able to fix the problems, and the management was getting desperate to turn the company around. When Don visited the office he saw all the

telltale signs. Discouraged people, a general
lack of energy and possibly the most
impressive array of pain relievers ever
assembled on display in the mailroom.

Don was running a smaller company with
an excellent reputation. People of the
highest quality in the field were always
expressing a desire to work for Don.

"Aha," thought Don, "a simple turnaround.
I'll take over the key department, hire the
best people, and turn it around in six months."

Don had just gone through Steps One, Two,
Three and Four:

Step One: "I have a problem." (I'm feeling
some discomfort.)

Step Two: "This is the problem." (Things
aren't the way I expect them to be.)

Step Three: "Here are some possible
solutions." (This should get things back to
the way I want them to be.)

Step Four: "This is the best solution."
(This looks like it will fix things without
causing me any more discomfort.)

So, with great fanfare and publicity, Don
took over the key department at the new
company. Then, when he began to
implement his solution, **Step Five:** "I'll try
this one," (Take action) he ran into an
unexpected barrier.

Not one of the people who were so
interested in working for Don at his old
company, had the slightest desire to work at
the new company.

"It's a joke," one man told him. "Not only
would I not work at a place with that bad of
a reputation, but I think you're a fool to
go there."

So Don encountered a huge barrier,
rendering his plan useless in its present
form.

HOW DON WON.

At this point Don could have taken the path
that many of us do. He could have easily
given up, returned to his old company or
just stayed as long as he could at the new
one. He could have blamed others, justified
his failure and defended the mediocrity of
the new company

Instead, he won. Don added Steps Six,
Seven and Eight.

Step Six: "Here are some possible solutions
to the barrier." (When I get past my
disappointment, this problem isn't so hard.)

Possible Solution 1:
I can go to other cities and bring people in
who don't know about the company's
reputation.

Possible Solution 2:
I can pick the best people already here and
train them.

Possible Solution 3:
I can do a lot of the work myself and get the
quality up.

Step Seven: "This is the best solution."
(I'll make sure the original problem still
gets solved.)

Don chose a combination of 2 and 3:
I can pick the best people already here and
train them. And I can do a lot of the work
myself and get the quality up, which will
also model for the people I'm training.

Then Don went to **Step Eight:** He repeated
Step Five "I'll try this one" (Take action.)
through Step Eight until he was out of
discomfort.

This meant that every day, as he
implemented his solutions, more barriers
came up. So he just treated them as new
problems to create opportunities until before
long he had accomplished his goal.

During the first year his people began to
win industry awards for the quality of their
work. This then attracted the attention of the
people who had turned Don down to work
there. Soon, several of them saw the
changes and joined the company after all.

So solving the barriers (improve the quality)
actually implemented a solution that made
Don's first solution (hire better people)
workable.

The company began to attract new business
and grew to double their size in two-and-a-
half years. Don accomplished his
turnaround and had a great time doing it.
All because he saw beyond the normal
problem-solving steps to the hidden steps,
and took action on them.

And now, you can, too.

Part III
HOW TO BE A CREATOR.

Chapter Eight.
HOW TO SEE BEYOND YOUR PROBLEM.

"In order for a proposition to be capable of being true, it must also be capable of being false."
– Ludwig Wittgenstein

It's as simple as this: Think of the most obvious truths about your problem, then state their opposites.

Gregory Heisler, the visionary New York photographer who does covers for Time magazine, New York Times magazine and others, uses this principle to blow away problems and reach a new level of creation in many aspects of his work.

"When the lighting isn't working, I do the opposite," says Heisler.

"Most people start with the light that's already there. I turn off everything and start with darkness. That usually gives me a new insight on what I'm really trying to say in my photograph."

"Then, if I'm still not satisfied, I do another opposite. I'll put the lights in back that should normally be in front. And vice versa. Often this will produce a completely unusual effect focusing on just the thing that I want it to."

Heisler's work has won international acclaim. And yet he says, "It's not about film and lenses. This is just a small part of it. Rather it's about communicating in ways that break the molds and clichés. Without this principle of opposites, I couldn't do it nearly as well."

In another situation, Ted Loken, Chairman of Measured Marketing, Inc., and a nationally recognized expert on direct marketing, had a problem: Because so many companies saw the growth potential in direct marketing, Ted got frequent calls to come and teach these other companies how to get into the business, and how to make it work for them.

He saw it as an increasing problem, because traveling to another company pulled him off the work at hand, and educating the competition didn't seem to lead to anything positive for his company.

Ted then put the principle of Obvious Opposites to work for him.

THE OBVIOUS: Consulting with other companies does little for us.

THE OPPOSITE: Consulting with other companies does a lot for us.

How could this be true?

For Ted, the answer was quite revealing. "For one thing, getting out of my own day-to-day work forces me to take a broader look at what we're doing. And it's much easier to learn that from someone else's company, where I'm not so emotionally attached, and then apply it to ours once I have the answer.

So in a sense, they're paying me to work at my own business.

For another thing, they pay me right away.
Which is the opposite of most of our
projects where the clients often pay when
the work is all done. So, the more of this
kind of work I do, the more it improves our
cash flow.

Sometimes these so-called competitors see
that we can do things they can't and actually
become our customers. Which is another
way this activity builds our business.

And finally, I never return from one of these
trips without a renewed sense of confidence.
Learning how little these other companies
know helps me reaffirm the tremendous
value we create in the market."

"So, yes," says Ted Loken, "it's a terrible
waste of time when I go out consulting with
our competition. And it's a fabulous waste
of time."

HOW TO CREATE THE BUSINESS OF YOUR DREAMS.

If you haven't yet created the business of your dreams, you can use the principle of opposites to create it for you.

The steps are simple:

1. OUTCOME. State the business you want to be in.

2. OBVIOUS. State the most obvious thing about that business.

3. OPPOSITE. State the opposite of that most obvious thing about that business.

4. "OPPOTUNITY." State how the opposite of that most obvious thing can be true. (OPPOTUNITY IS A "<u>UNITY</u>" OF "<u>OPPO</u>SITES").

William E. Weisman, a successful and innovative Minneapolis businessman and member of the Young President's Organization (YPO), used just this kind of thinking when he started his business about 10 years ago.

First, he chose the vending business for two reasons.

1. He knew it well.
2. No one was innovating.

From this he created a company that revolutionized the way retailers do business with vending companies.

Weisman's thinking looked something like this:

1. OUTCOME. State the business you want to be in. THE VENDING BUSINESS.

2. OBVIOUS. State the most obvious thing about that business. VEND MEANS "SELL."

3. OPPOSITE. State the opposite of that most obvious thing about that business. VEND MEANS "BUY."

4. "OPPOTUNITY." State how the opposite of that most obvious thing can be true.

VENDING COMPANIES HAVE ALWAYS SOLD THINGS TO RETAILERS, BUT HAVE NEVER BOUGHT THINGS FOR RETAILERS.

Out of this "oppotunity" came Best Vendors, Inc., the first vending management company. Instead of selling machines to the retailers, he went to them and said: "I'll manage your vending program so that you'll get more out of it. I'll hire the vending contractors for you, manage the contracts and present you with a check at the end of every quarter, most likely for more than you're getting out of it now."

Weisman's first customer was the giant retailer, Target Stores, Inc. It worked so well for them that others followed in rapid succession.

In fact, Best Vendors, Inc., is now an industry leader in the overall area of vending, having created the first national vending company, with sales in excess of $100 million.

HOMER HANKY HANKY-PANKY.

In 1991 The Minnesota Twins won the World Series for the second time in five years. Four of the seven games were played in the Hubert Humphrey Metrodome, home of the Homer Hanky.

The hanky, brainchild of Teri Robins, Promotion Director of the Minneapolis Star Tribune, fast became the symbol of rabid fans in the Dome.

The Homer Hanky created a new category of team-imprinted items. Rather than wearing this product, you wave it, especially when your team hits a home run.

How to invent a successful new product: think of the Opposite of the Obvious.

1. OUTCOME. Create a new Homer Hanky for baseball fans.

2. OBVIOUS. A Homer Hanky is for the best thing you can do in baseball. (A home run.)

3. OPPOSITE. A Homer Hanky is for the worst thing you can do in baseball. (A strikeout.)

4. "OPPOTUNITY." (State how the opposite of that most obvious thing can be true.)

From this came the realization that the Homer Hanky was only good for half the game. After all, you wouldn't wave a Homer Hanky at the other team and have them hit a home run, would you?

Thus was invented the answer to the Homer Hanky: THE 1991 STRIKEOUT SNOTRAG.

It also used several other opposites. The Homer Hanky was wholesome; the Strikeout Snotrag was unwholesome.

The Homer Hanky was red, the Strikeout Snotrag green. Why green? Syd Thrift, former General Manager of the Pittsburgh Pirates, in his book, *The Game According to Syd,* explains the research of a certain Dr. Ott, who found that the color green tended to weaken baseball players, and the colors blue and gray didn't. This research led to many major league fences being painted blue, and the undersides of the caps changing from green to gray.

So, theoretically, the green hanky, waved in mass quantities at the opposing team, could weaken them enough to cause a strikeout. Did it work?

The 1991 World Series had only 16 Homers and 87 Strikeouts. (I rest my case.)

OPPOSITES CREATE BREAKTHROUGH THINKING EVERYWHERE.

The only difference between humor and creativity is that in humor the elements don't blend into a new truth. For example, one source of humor is redefining everyday buzz words. The more you hear them, the better targets they are.

When I first heard the saucy term "unauthorized biography," I asked what was obvious about it.

It was obvious that an unauthorized
biography is written by someone the subject
would not cooperate with.

The opposite of that is someone the subject
would cooperate with.

That person would be one's self. Or
expressed in unity with the original term:
I've written an Unauthorized
Autobiography.

MUSIC. Music is made up of many
opposites. One of the best examples, when
one of the great masters was asked what the
difference was between a good symphony
and a great one;

It was obvious music is made up of notes.

The opposite: music is made up of
everything that's not the notes.

"What makes a great symphony," replied
the master, "are the spaces between the notes."

FILM. One of the hidden causes of power in many films is the sound track. This alone is an opposite, because we rely so heavily on our visual senses in film. Imagine you are scoring the music for a film with a murder scene. Your job: to make that murder scene more horrible than any before it. A big job.

It is obvious that murder scenes are played to scary music.

The opposite is that murder scenes are played to happy music.

And there you have the inspiration for some of the powerful scenes from *A Clockwork Orange*, where the leader of the gang was stomping and kicking one of his victims to the happy tune of "Singin' In The Rain."

Horror films have also used opposites like kids, clowns and other happy symbols to make the horror more horrible.

Successful romantic films establish a context of rejection to make the ultimate "boy gets girl" or acceptance more powerful.

Comedies are often based on their own opposite: human suffering. It works especially well when the person doing the suffering represents someone we perceive to be in a higher place in society than we are.

Again this shows a unity of opposites, as in someone from a high place falling down.

Chapter Nine
FOUR STEPS TO OWNING YOUR CREATIVITY.

"Nothing in the universe can travel at the speed of light, they say, forgetful of the shadow's speed."
– Howard Nemerov

1. OUTCOME.
2. OBVIOUS.
3. OPPOSITE.
4. "OPPOTUNITY."

These four steps are your keys to harnessing the power of opposites and having Innovation on Demand for the rest of your life. But beware. Just like your experience of riding a bicycle for the first time, this process can seem a bit awkward at first. And just like the bike, don't give up. After you've done this a few times and created some powerful results, it will get easier and easier. In fact, many people now do it unconsciously, and use the steps to make sure they're on the right track.

1. OUTCOME. Write a simple sentence describing anything you want to solve or accomplish.

☞ Write this in the form of a "do what to whom," "do what with whom" or a "do what for whom" statement.

Example: Sell 4-wheel drive cars to women.

Example: Invent hair replacement for balding men.

Now your outcome statement is an objective or goal, stated always with "what" and "whom."

☞ Highlight the two key words (the nouns describing "what" and "whom.")

Example 1: Sell <u>4-wheel drive cars</u> to <u>women.</u>

Example 2: Invent <u>hair replacement</u> for <u>balding men.</u>

2. OBVIOUS. Select the three most obvious aspects of each of the key words.

☞ Play the word association game with each highlighted word to get the three most obvious associations.

Example: 4-wheel drive cars = Off road, tough, powerful.
Women = Pretty, gentle, mothers.

☞ Construct another simple sentence showing the relationship between (the Outcome) and (the Obvious).

Example: 4-wheel drive cars go off road.

Example: 4-wheel drive cars are tough.

Example: 4-wheel drive cars are powerful.

Example: Women are pretty.

Example: Women are gentle.

Example: Women are mothers.

☞ Now, you do the same with examples two and three.

3. OPPOSITE. Insert the Opposite of the Obvious into each sentence to create a contradiction.

☞ Write the opposite of each obvious association you created in the last step.

Example: (4-wheel drive cars)
Obvious association = Off road.
Opposite = On road, to the opera.

Obvious association = Tough.
Opposite = Vulnerable, tender.

Obvious association = Powerful.
Opposite = Weak, wimpy.

Example: (Women)
Obvious association = Pretty.
Opposite = Ugly, handsome.

Obvious association = Gentle.
Opposite = Rough, wild.

Obvious association = Mothers.
Opposite = Fathers, children.

☞ Take the simple sentence showing the relationship between the Outcome and the Obvious and substitute the Opposite for the Obvious, thereby creating a contradiction.

Example: 4-wheel drive cars go on road.

Example: 4-wheel drive cars go to the opera.

Example: 4-wheel drive cars are vulnerable.

Example: 4-wheel drive cars are tender.

Example: 4-wheel drive cars are weak.

Example: 4-wheel drive cars are wimpy.

Example: Women are ugly.

Example: Women are handsome.

Example: Women are rough.

Example: Women are wild.

Example: Women are fathers.

Example: Women are children.

☞Now, you do the same with examples two and three.

4. "OPPOTUNITY." Look at each of your contradictions and ask "How could this be true?" The answer will produce your "oppotunity" (again, an opportunity caused by a unity of opposites.)

☞ Example: 4-wheel drive cars go on road. How could this be true? Well, since 4-wheel drive cars spend most of their time on the road anyway, this suggests more of a mainstream car. Just the thing for a woman caught in a storm or other driving hazard. Own a 4-wheel drive car and you know you'll be safe.

☞ Example: 4-wheel drive cars go to the opera. How could this be true? This contradiction suggests an elegant car, one

with all the comfort and luxury of a town
car, but all the ruggedness of an off-road
car.

☞ Now, you do the same with the apparent
contradiction: "Women are fathers."

THE ONLY WAY TO LEARN HOW TO RIDE A BIKE: STAY ON THE BIKE.

Now try it on your own. See how quickly
you can reach a powerful new truth with this
four-step method. If you run into trouble,
just refer to the prior examples. Let's do a
really tough problem, because with
opposites your solution will be all the more
powerful.

You've heard the old saying: "He's such a
good salesman, he can sell refrigerators to
Eskimos." Well, that's your assignment.
Remember:

1. OUTCOME.
2. OBVIOUS.
3. OPPOSITE.
4. "OPPOTUNITY."

Try it, then read on for the answer.

1. OUTCOME. Sell refrigerators to Eskimos.

2. OBVIOUS.
a. Refrigerators keep things cool.
b. Eskimos live in the North.

3. OPPOSITE.
a. Refrigerators keep things warm.
b. Eskimos live in the South.

4. "OPPOTUNITY."
a. A refrigerator's insulation keeps food from freezing.
b. Two Eskimos move to Phoenix. Sell them a refrigerator for their condo (instead of their igloo.)

Chapter Ten
INNOVATION ON DEMAND: APPLY IT ANYWHERE.

"We can't leave the haphazard to chance."
— N.F Simpson

The following are some of the results accomplished by people who have learned the Innovation on Demand method.

Check the areas that interest you and imagine all the powerful ideas you could quickly produce and problems you could easily solve.

1. Quality. If you're doing a quality programming of your business, use Innovation on Demand to make leaps to improvement rather than just plodding steps.

For example, an insurance company was addressing a phone problem. Too many phone calls were coming in, and, therefore, callers had to hold for longer than acceptable periods of time.

Traditional management thinking would result in more phones and more people to answer them. This, then, could often lead to even less efficiency in the system with new equipment and new people, causing even longer waits.

So instead of changing equipment, why not change the thinking?

Here's what the group came up with:
1. OUTCOME. (Do what to whom?)
Improve phone system for customers.

2. OBVIOUS.

A. Phone system must handle *more* calls.
B. Customers need information.

3. OPPOSITE.

A. Phone system must handle *fewer* calls.
B. Customers don't need information.

4. "OPPOTUNITY." (How could this be true?)

A. Find out the main reasons for calls and give the people the information before they have to call for it.
B. Customers don't need to call for the information if they already have it.

So, here is an idea that can, if implemented, save the company lots of money: The cost of new equipment plus the cost of new people plus the cost of training them. What's better? The new idea (finding out the most common questions customers have, then answering them in advance) will not only cost much less but will also produce a much more efficient phone system. Because it lessens the stress on what the people already know how to do with the equipment already in place.

So, think of Innovation on Demand as a powerful new tool for the quality processes in your company. Without it, this insurance company may never have reached the key distinction that allowed them to eliminate the root cause of the problem, rather than, as so many companies do, adding more phones and people.

2. New Products. In the pet food category, it was obvious almost all products treated pets as *inferior* creatures.

The opposite of that was treating them as *superior* creatures.

Thus was born Haute Canine, the Gourmet Dog Snack. Notice the unity of opposites: The words Haute Canine sound and look like Haute Cuisine, creating a unity of the words, yet combining the opposites of gourmet and dog.

"How could this contradiction be true?" Through pet lovers' well-known psychological transference of love, that would normally be given to children, to their pets. This idea is often used to explain the pampered pets who are treated better than humans.

Yet, despite widespread knowledge of this pampered pet syndrome, there were no products that catered to this type of owner, especially in the pet snack area.

Capitalizing on this "oppotunity," Linda Coffey of L. Coffey Ltd. created Haute Canine and its sister product, Haute Feline, for cats, a multi-million dollar line of pet products sold through the finest stores and catalogs.

3. Life planning. In one woman's life, it was obvious her goals were all centered around *business*.

The opposite: Her goals were *personal*.

When she asked how that could be true, she realized what she really wanted in her life was to be married. But somehow she'd given up on that and convinced herself that what she wanted was a successful business career.

She immediately shifted her focus from business to personal, and a short time later met the man to whom she is now married. She said, "Without this shift in thinking, I'd be single today and unhappily successful in business."

4. **Job Advancement.** Another user of this method tells of teaching it to a client who was ready to fire his sales manager.

It was obvious much of what the sales manager was doing was *not working*.

The opposite was that much of what he was doing *was working*.

How could this be true? Nothing is ever completely good or bad. And yet, due to the mind's clinging tendency to fill any communication gaps with negative thought, it's often possible for a boss to see only one side of the story about an employee.

The solution: seeing the previously hidden positive side.

Soon after, the client experienced a dramatic turnaround in his opinion of the sales manager. Eventually, he promoted his "disappointing" sales manager to Vice President, Sales.

Chapter Eleven
OUTCOME: HOW TO GET WHAT YOU WANT.

"Reality can destroy the dream, why shouldn't the dream destroy reality?"
– George Moore

The first contradiction: If you want something, don't start at the beginning. Start at the end. That's why the first step is the outcome. Start with anything that's not now happening, but that you'd like to happen.

Let's say you're in business selling sweaters to young mothers. Your outcome statement would then be: Sell more sweaters to young mothers.

Or you're a supplier to other companies. Your outcome statement might be: Get more orders from Fortune 500 companies.

Or, outcome: Serve more meals to business people.

Notice that each of these statements has a subject and an object, as in "Do WHAT to WHOM." The subjects: sweaters, orders, meals. The objects: young mothers, Fortune 500 companies, business people.

We do this for two reasons. First, if your desired outcome is new business, you need to get this new business from somewhere. Acknowledging *where* in your outcome statement is the first step in getting it. And second, a subject and an object make you be specific in your outcome statement.

But back to reason one. You improve your performance by focusing on the person who can deliver that improvement for you. Unfortunately, most of us focus only on the product rather than on the person who is going to use it. This keeps us from most of our opportunities.

For example, let's be outrageous. Imagine that you want to put an intercontinental ballistic missile in your front yard. Now this would most likely be impossible. After all, these missiles are under the most stringent security.

And yet, I'll bet you that you could do it. All you need to do is have the cooperation of the right people. Start with the President of the United States. "I just want this ICBM in my yard for awhile. Let's aim it at...oh, I don't know, maybe Upper Volta."

Now the President is the Commander-In-Chief. That's a good start in getting an OK.

Why can we accomplish so much by focusing on people? Let's look at what motivates. Reader's Digest, being in the business of condensing books and articles, ran a test to find out what people thought was short copy and long copy. This test was motivated by the thought that if something was too long, people wouldn't read it. (This is borne out by advertising readership scores where, on the average, 93 percent of the readers don't read more than half the words.)

First they showed the test subjects some copy that was labeled 25 words long and some labeled 2,500 words long. The subjects naturally identified 25 words as short copy and 2,500 words as long copy.

THE READER'S DIGEST SHORT COPY/LONG COPY TEST.
This is the time for all good men to come to the aid of the party.
SHORT COPY.
LONG COPY.

Then, they added another variable. They titled one copy block with the name of another person, and the other copy block, "Me." Let's assume that you, the reader, and I, the author, are doing this test. With this new variable, you are told the 25 words are about Allen Fahden, the author, and the 2,500 words are about you, the reader.

If you are at all like the subjects in this Reader's Digest test, you would say, "25 words about him? No, I got bored about half way through and stopped reading."

Then you'd say "2500 words about me? Very interesting, but you forgot the part about when I was scissors monitor in fifth grade. And could you just add a little about the time I..."

Conclusion: If you want to interest someone in getting you to your outcome, you must focus on them, because "I" am most interested in "me."

By starting with the outcome, then, you focus the rest of your thinking on your

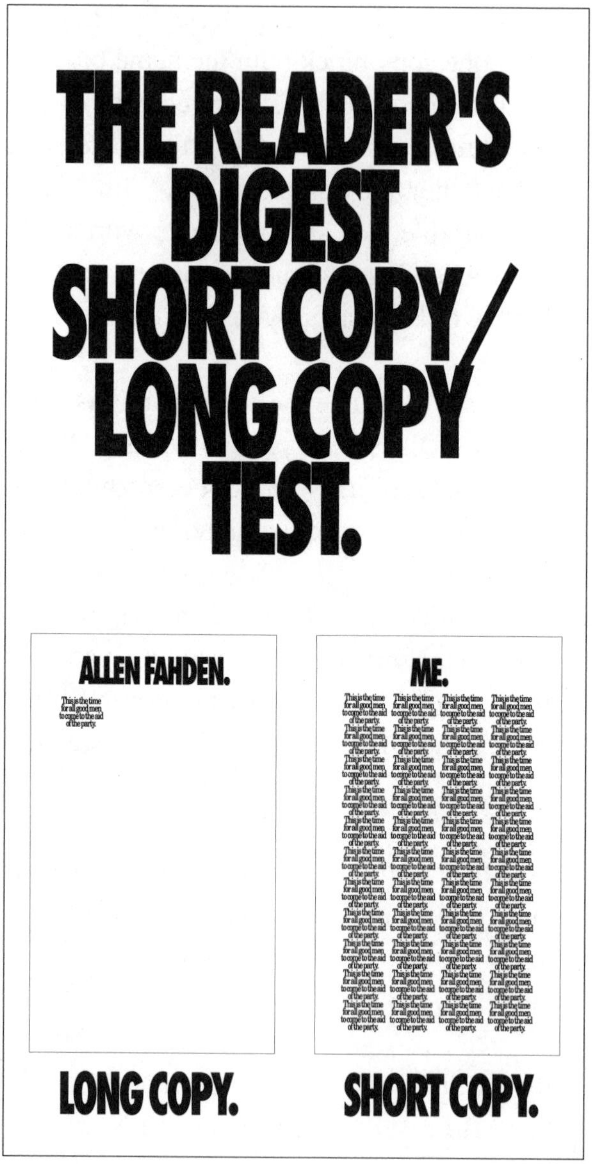
THE READER'S
DIGEST
SHORT COPY/
LONG COPY
TEST.
ALLEN FAHDEN.
This is the time for all good men to come to the aid of the party.
ME.
This is the time for all good men to come to the aid of the party.
LONG COPY.
SHORT COPY.

target audience, the customers whose attention you want to attract. The next steps in the process show how you can creatively capture their attention and get above the noise.

HOW TO GET THE BEST OUTCOME STATEMENT.

To make the best outcome statement, you need to pay attention to two key criteria.

1. The content of the statement.

2. The structure of the statement.

Obviously, the content of the outcome must clearly state what you want to accomplish.

THE CONTENT OF THE OUTCOME STATEMENT.

This step alone could create tremendous value, because in business as in life, many people are not exactly sure what they want to accomplish.

If you are not sure, focus on what outcome inspires you the most.

If you're in it for the money, fine. Then your outcome statement should express it. OUTCOME: "Earn a million dollars from car buyers."

If your outcome words are especially familiar, play the "word association game" for evoking the most widely held beliefs.

Example:
WORD: Million Dollars.

ASSOCIATION: Rich.

WORD: Car Buyers.

ASSOCIATION: Wary.

More in the next chapter under the OBVIOUS step.

THE STRUCTURE OF THE OUTCOME STATEMENT.

Now, put that content in a "do what to whom" form.

OUTCOME: "Sell dry cleaning to families."

OUTCOME: "Deliver motivational message to sales force."

You can also create an outcome statement that does something for, with or from someone.

OUTCOME: "Secure financing for start-up company."

OUTCOME: "Create joint venture with prosperous partner."

OUTCOME: "Cut expenses from budget."

WHY "WHAT" AND "WHOM?"

Why do you need a two-part statement? Why not just say, "cut expenses?"

Well, you can. But you'll miss out on more than half the power. After all, you can't

change a lot about the *concept* of cutting
expenses. But you can change how you act
in the *context* of cutting expenses.

That's why the person who decides your
fate is such a necessary part of your power
to create. Combine that with your subject,
and you've created a fertile beginning.

THE DIFFICULTY/VALUE FACTOR.

One last criterion in selecting your outcome:
Not only should this outcome be something
you want, but the more difficult it is to
accomplish, the better.

In fact, if what you want is impossible,
Innovation on Demand is just the thing for
you. That's because, *the more difficult
something is to accomplish, the more easy
its opposite will make it.*

So, by all means, pick the most difficult
outcome to achieve. Especially if people say
it can't be done.

HOW TO FIND OUT WHAT YOU WANT IF YOU DON'T KNOW WHAT YOU WANT.

It's almost epidemic. Ask people what they want and many will say something general like, "I want to be happy." The problem with that is the only way you can get it is simply to be happy. Yet, most people depend on external circumstances to determine whether they'll be happy or not.

Unfortunately, they're like rudderless ships, moving from event to event, sometimes happy, sometimes not.

HOW TO BE HAPPY AND HOW TO KNOW WHAT YOU WANT ARE THE SAME THING.

The only way to get what you want is to be specific. So first, you have to know what you want. The good news: The way to find out what you want is to ask these two questions:

1. What am I good at?

2. What do I love to do?

Put these answers together and you'll know what you want. If, then, you can do what you're good at, you'll build your self-worth. If you can do what you love to do, you'll live a joyful life. So, with self-worth and joy, it will be hard not to be happy. For more on this read *You Can Have It All* by Arnold M. Patent. These ideas are based on his methods for finding your life's purpose.

If you aren't sure what you want, go through these steps and find out. Then you'll have the outcomes that can deliver the most value.

And then you can use Innovation on Demand to *get* what you want.

Now move to the next chapter to learn more about the OBVIOUS step in the four-step Innovation On Demand process.

USE THIS WORKSHEET TO WRITE YOUR CONCERNS.

The purpose for defining your concerns:
To lead to any action that will contribute value.

VALUE LEGEND.	DIFFICULTY LEGEND.
+ Great Value.	+ Very Difficult.
0 Some Value.	0 Somewhat Difficult.
- Little Value.	- Not Difficult.

WRITE YOUR CONCERNS HERE:

	Value	Difficulty
1.		
2.		
3.		
4.		
5.		
6.		
7.		

USE THIS WORKSHEET TO PUT YOUR CONCERNS IN THE CORRECT QUADRANTS.

Start with the highest item that's the farthest to the right. Then move from here to your Outcome Statement.

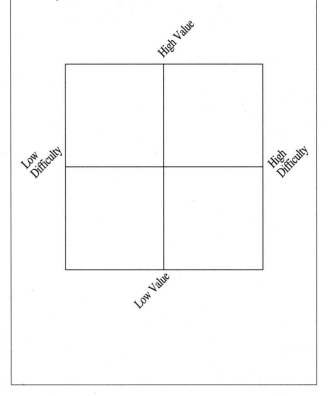

AN EXAMPLE OF RATING YOUR CONCERNS ON THE VALUE AND DIFFICULTY OF SOLVING THEM.

The purpose for defining your concerns:
To lead to any action that will contribute value.

VALUE LEGEND.	DIFFICULTY LEGEND.
+ Great Value.	+ Very Difficult.
0 Some Value.	0 Somewhat Difficult.
- Little Value.	- Not Difficult.

EXAMPLES:

	Value	Difficulty
1. Our phone customers have to wait too long on hold.	+	0
2. The market's not excited about our new products.	+	+
3. We keep running out of labels.	0	-
4.		
5.		
6.		
7.		

USE THIS WORKSHEET TO CONSTRUCT AN OUTCOME STATEMENT THAT WORKS.

1. Choose your top concerns from the top right quadrant.

2. Rewrite them into this form:

_____

(Verb)   (Noun)   (Preposition)   (Noun)

_____

(Verb)   (Noun)   (Preposition)   (Noun)

_____

(Verb)   (Noun)   (Preposition)   (Noun)

_____

(Verb)   (Noun)   (Preposition)   (Noun)

AN EXAMPLE OF CONVERTING YOUR CONCERNS TO OUTCOME STATEMENTS.

A useful Outcome Statement is vital to the process.

1. It must be clear.
2. It must represent a difficult and valuable concern.
3. It must contain two nouns. (i.e. Sell refrigerators to Eskimos.)
4. Each noun must evoke several word associations. (Paradigms.)
5. Adjectives are OK to describe nouns, but the adjective and noun must be treated as one idea to evoke word associations. (i.e. Sell electric refrigerators to Eskimos.)

EXAMPLES, from concerns page:

REDUCE	HOLD TIME	OF	PHONE CUSTOMERS.
(Verb)	(Noun)	(Preposition)	(Noun)

EXCITE	MARKET	ABOUT	NEW PRODUCTS.
(Verb)	(Noun)	(Preposition)	(Noun)

GUARANTEE	LABELS	FOR	CUSTOMERS.
(Verb)	(Noun)	(Preposition)	(Noun)

Chapter Twelve
THE OBVIOUS: IT CAN BE BLINDING.

"A little unlearning goes a long way."
    – Richard Kehl

The obstinate obvious is composed of all the judgments we've made about the people and things in this world. "Grass is green." "The sky is blue." "Foreigners are not to be trusted." On the positive side, the obvious helps us live in this world. On the negative side, the obvious limits us from seeing what's really there.

How to experience the obvious:

Here's a two-sentence story: Mary heard the bell. With birthday money in hand, Mary ran down the stairs.

Now close your eyes and visualize the story. What do you see? How much of what you visualized was in the original story? How old is Mary? Most people I've tried this with say five to eight years old. Many see her living in a white house with a picket fence and lots of trees. What was she wearing? Some say a party dress. Others saw shorts.

Actually, Mary is 72 and lives in a trailer in Arizona. And the bell could be a fire alarm. See all the items people put into the story that weren't there? Rather, their minds plugged these details into the story, based on their own frames of reference.

You have just experienced your own obstinate obvious, or in other words, your own way of seeing reality. The obstinate obvious is created by our own social conditioning, and, therefore, it's reality as you see it.

At this stage in your life your mind is pretty full of the obstinate obvious. And well it should be. In fact, without the obvious, how could you survive in this culture? Obvious thoughts like "Don't cross the street without looking both ways," are very useful. Yet, for your creativity, you need to go beyond them. Step one: identify them.

Try another brief story: A man runs home; another man is wearing a mask.

What is going on here? What do you think it is? If you're like many people, you'd guess a robber, Halloween or a masquerade party. This story, however, describes a baseball game. The baserunner is running home and the catcher, still wearing his mask, waits at home for him.

When we learn a business, the most important thing we can learn is the obstinate obvious, how it's done. Yet that's where most people stop. Many of us think, "I'll do my job and be good," hoping that will get us ahead. The true movers and shakers of the business world, however, are those who identify the obstinate obvious and make major changes. After all, the world remembers Neil Armstrong, the first man to walk on the moon. But who was the second? The fourth?

The point is that obvious things are our tools for survival in our culture, but we don't have to let them limit us.

Sociologist Thomas Kuhn found that
scientists–people who are supposed to be
among the most objective in our
culture–were just as victimized by their
obstinate obvious as you and I are by ours.
In fact, they dealt quite differently with
information that supported the scientific
thought of the day than they did with
information that didn't. When supportive
data came in, they would test it, analyze it,
reorganize it and write lots of papers. But
when data came in that didn't support the
scientific theory of the day, they would
ignore it.

Perhaps that is why Copernicus' idea the
Earth revolves around the sun was treated
with such contempt, and even why it was
such a shock when it was proved the Earth
was actually round.

THE ONLY THINGS THAT KEEP YOUR BUSINESS FROM MOVING AHEAD ARE THE FACTS YOU CAN'T YET LEAVE BEHIND.

So, why should you be even slightly concerned with the obstinate obvious? You'd think an astute business person is one who deals only in the facts, or at least the facts as he or she sees them. Yet the most astute business people are those who have done just the opposite.

Fact 1980: Chrysler Corporation may soon be out of the car business.

Fact 1993: Chrysler Corporation is still alive.

If Lee Iacocca had accepted the fact that Chrysler could make only second rate cars and was perpetually a government bailout candidate, Chrysler most likely would still be there. Yet in Iacocca's vision he saw an even more powerful truth. And then he acted to make it happen: He led the Chrysler Corporation from losses to profit.

CREATIVITY: THE DEFEAT OF HABIT BY THE IMAGINATION.

What Iacocca did was creatively challenge the facts of the situation. In other words, he forced a huge corporation to break its habits. The habit of creating unexciting cars. The habit of doing things the "way they're supposed to be done." The habit of holding their heads down instead of up.

After all, that's what many facts are: habits that we don't challenge. Just as individuals are creatures of habit, so, too, are companies, rarely challenging where they are or why they do what they do, until absolutely forced to.

And today, increasingly, many companies in many industries are being seriously challenged by outside forces. Too often, though, their habits, or their reading of the "facts," keep them from meeting those challenges head on.

If you stick with the facts, you'll be stuck with them when they become untruths.

Facts that were true yesterday don't always remain true. As stated before in the introduction, there are two kinds of changes: structural and cyclical.

When a change is structural, like the atomic bomb or the automobile, it means we never return to the way it was before the structural change. When the change is cyclical, like fashion or interest rates, it means you can depend on some kind of return to the way things were before.

Unfortunately, many people believe that almost all changes are structural. For example, the person who has just undergone a change that produces success will often keep doing that same change over and over, even after it no longer works. This will have them blindly making business decisions based on evaporating facts, or, perhaps, buying into a company right at the top and then suffering at the sudden drop in value.

A fact is only a widely held notion of the obstinate obvious. The more widely held, the bigger your "oppotunity."

The idea that most changes are cyclical doesn't have to hurt you. It can also help you. All you need to do is understand where in the cycle things are.

The first step: Look at the "facts." These are not real truths; they are simply the obvious, or the way we see reality.

Maybe one of the first obstinate obvious ideas you ever learned in business was "Bigger Is Better." If you added to that phrase/statement/belief the experience of losing business to some of the giants who could offer a better product, price or service, you may even have learned that lesson bitterly. So now you have more than just a phrase/statement/belief and its meaning. You have a connected chain of thoughts. And because the mind works much like a computer, those connections will remain there until you program new ones.

THE MAN WHO TURNED A WHOLE ORGANIZATION UPSIDE DOWN.

Consider: Jan Carlzon, president of the Scandinavian airline SAS, was a wizard at using the obstinate obvious to his company's advantage. In his book, *Moments of Truth*, he described an industry where the obvious was: Big planes allowed you to carry more people efficiently on fewer flights and concentrate on vacation travelers.

But Carlzon looked around. What he saw were a lot of business travelers in the Scandinavian countries needing to make frequent, short trips to other Scandinavian and European cities. SAS then targeted these travelers, putting more money into promotions aimed at them than at vacationers. The airline bought smaller planes and instituted more frequent, short hops.

SAS grew as business people realized that they could board a plane in the morning in Oslo, for example, fly to Hamburg for a meeting, and then fly home that evening.

While these shifts proved highly beneficial
for SAS, perhaps one of the most dramatic
shifts that Carlzon made was inverting the
corporate pyramid. Rather than have a few
at the top making the majority of the
decisions, he empowered the rank and file
to make most of them, those crucial ones
that involved the customers on a daily basis.

For example, if a customer missed a flight
or got bumped, it was the counter clerk who
could issue a voucher for a meal, or put the
customer up for the night, or get him on a
competitor's airline. Carlzon included these
decisions in what he called "moments of
truth." In other words, when you're
approached by a customer with a question
or complaint, how you handle that moment
adds to the credibility of the company. If the
customer had lost his luggage, then an
employee did everything possible to locate
it and get it to the customer as quickly
as possible.

While most corporations have some form of
long-range plan they feel is imperative,
whether it is a five-year, two-year, or one-

year plan, Carlzon saw the "moments of truth" as the most important aspect to doing business. And allowing front-line employees to make the crucial customer decisions freed Carlzon and his top staff to become the visionaries, thinking of where SAS could go, and how it would get there, way down the road.

HOW TO MAKE THE OBSTINATE OBVIOUS WORK FOR YOU.

Once you've created a workable outcome statement (see the last chapter for details), you're ready for step two: the OBVIOUS. Start with the words that most obviously go together with the nouns in your OUTCOME statement. (Look for the "what" and "whom" as the nouns in your Do What To Whom OUTCOME statement.)

Hint: Play the "Word Association Game." You remember: one person says a word, you say the first word that pops into your mind. "Sky. Blue." "Dog. Cat." "Stove. Hot."

Then once you have a few words, pick the most obvious. For example, lets say your outcome statement is, "Sell products to people." And your most obvious association with "product" is the word "manufacture."

Why?

Well, for one thing, this word is the most universal. Or put another way:

1. Choose an association with the fewest exceptions.
Products are manufactured. They are not created from air.
2. Choose an association that people accept without question.

Almost without question production of products involves manufacturing.

WORDS ALONE WILL NEVER COMMUNICATE THE OBVIOUS.

Next step. Very important. Put each obvious word into a sentence that associates it with the noun it came from in the OUTCOME statement. EXAMPLE: Products are manufactured.

Why a sentence? Because you're building a context or framework in which to insert your opposite. If you go from "cold" to "hot," that does you no good.

But if you go from "Refrigerators keep things cold" to "Refrigerators keep things hot," now you have a contradiction. And that contradiction is the launching pad for your creativity.

It's just like the idea of high only being high in reference to the ground. And white is whitest in a field of black, as you saw in the first part of the book.

The power of your creativity lies in your ability to change the context. And the farther or more opposite that context is from the obvious, the more powerful your creativity.

So, move to the next chapter for the power
of opposites.

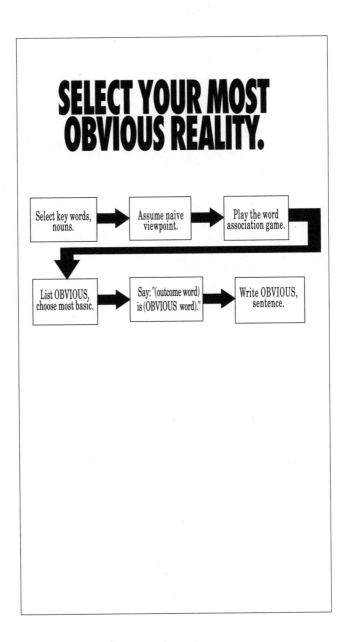

Chapter Thirteen
THE OPPOSITE: LEARNING TO RIDE THE CYCLES

"The greatest enemy of any one of our truths may be the rest of our truths."
— William James

The human mind hates a paradox. That's because the mind craves order, and a paradox is about the most chaotic thing the mind can encounter. After all, if we define paradox to be two seemingly conflicting ideas in a single thought, no wonder the mind resists.

Yet, once again, the very weight of this problem creates the enormity of the "oppotunity."

Whether we like it or not, once we're faced with a paradox or a contradiction, our minds go into immediate action. Which means you can't help but come up with an answer. What's more, that answer, due to the distance you've traveled with your opposite, has got to be one you haven't seriously considered.

Some great truths that used to be contradictions:

The Earth is round. (To this day the Flat Earth Society still clings to the other notion).

The Earth revolves around the sun. (Copernicus was shunned and imprisoned for this revolutionary idea).

Consider: IBM was the largest seller of personal computers in the business market. What, then, was Apple, which coveted the same market, to do? Go head to head with Big Blue?

John Sculley, chairman of Apple, knew that would prove costly. He also instinctively knew how to use contradictions to creatively arrive at successful solutions. If IBM means business computers, what then would be the contradiction? The obvious about this: Before we all get into some kind of business, broadly defined, we are being educated. The contradiction, then, was IBM means educational computers. But of course, it didn't.

That, then, was Apple's "oppotunity." Apple entered the education market, selling, and often donating, thousands of its computers to colleges and high schools. Not only was the company using contradictions successfully, it was also borrowing a page out of the universal drivers education manual. Why have auto manufacturers provided so many cars for high school drivers education classes? For the simple reason that if a boy or girl learns to drive on a certain type of car, chances increase the man or woman will someday buy that car.

Tens of thousands of American students have learned on Apple computers. Today they are in business. And by the early 90's, Apple had surpassed IBM in selling personal computers to both the education and business markets.

HOW TO CREATE SOMETHING WHEN YOU CAN'T.

The more hopeless your situation, the more useful you'll find the Innovation On Demand method.

A large architectural firm applied this thinking to one of their toughest problems. They were stuck in the process of designing their own building.

Of course, this project was one of their most important, because it was an opportunity to showcase their best work in one of the most visible forms (their building.)

However, they had a sticky problem: Not enough money to build beyond the bare necessities of basic walls, electrical, heating and cooling and lighting.

Now contrast this problem with their stated objective: To build a building that places their firm on the leading edge of architecture.

Could the conflict be any more challenging?
The need to do something great, and no
money to do it. (How many times have you
faced this same conflict?)

What's more, every time they thought of an
idea, they had to scrap it because it was
addition to the space and therefore an
addition to the budget.

(Here's a clue: what's the opposite of
addition?)

It was obvious that traditional thinking was
getting them nowhere. So, together we
applied the Innovation On Demand method.

1. OUTCOME. Design an innovative building
for our people.

2. OBVIOUS. An innovative building is on
the leading edge.

3. OPPOSITE. An innovative building is in
the Stone Age.

4. "OPPOTUNITY." (State how the opposite
of that most obvious thing can be true.)

An innovative building is in the Stone Age
when it's designed for the way people in the
Stone Age operated. Because those people
live in tribes, the architectural firm used
tribal society as a model for their plans.
How could a tribe operate today? Look for
the unity with an idea that's already in
today's businesses, and you'll find that tribe
closely parallels the idea of team.

Now, go back to the most impossible part of
the problem. No budget beyond the bare
necessities. Using the model of tribe to
create a work space for their teams allowed
the architects to design to a completely
different budget need.

Instead of adding costly features to their
office, they subtracted some of the most
obvious and basic ones. After all, would a
tribe build walls to separate their people?
Then why should a team?

This allowed them to plan a space that
actually priced out under the bare
minimums. So what did they do with the
extra money to create a leading edge space?
They followed the model of tribe further,
and painted in visual symbols that make
their space unique and powerful.

So the Stone Age put them on the leading
edge.

Chapter Fourteen
"OPPOTUNITY." - A UNITY OF OPPOSITES.

"Between yea and nay, how much difference is there?"
 – Lao Tzu

"Rome wasn't built in a day."
 – Anon.

"Yeah, but parts of it were."
 – Anon.

Researchers used to believe that attitudes cause behavior: So if you changed the attitudes, you'd change the behavior: Yet in a recent study commissioned by a leading national magazine, just the opposite was found to be true. (What a surprise.) This study showed that to change an attitude or a belief, one must first change the behavior: Then, and only then, can the clinging mind let go of the old beliefs, spurred on by the newer, stronger motivation: to avoid looking stupid to others for not using the new behavior: In other words, we see here the principle of cognitive dissonance.

We behave from inner motivations, then we must go to any lengths to rationalize them to others. "The Ferrari? Oh, I bought it for the gas mileage."

So, if we want to make changes, there's only one way to do it. Make changes. The rest will follow, and things will get better.

And, if for some reason they don't, you can always make other changes.

The purpose of this book is to give you the opportunities to make the best changes you can.

Here's an opportunity for you. Start with the obvious: "When business gets bad, we have to cut prices." But make it about your business.

Now insert the opposite of any key words, like "when recreation gets good, we have to cut the price" or "when business gets good, we have to cut the price" or "when business gets bad we have to raise the price" or "when business gets bad we have to cut the inventory."

Can any of these statements be true for you or your business?

For instance, for some of us the example statement, "when recreation gets good, we have to cut the price," may be true in the sense that if we go play, we don't sell much. So we need to cut the price when we get back to getting things going again. This statement may be true, but unless too much play is your business problem, it won't be particularly helpful.

The statement, "when business gets good, we have to cut the price," might be an opportunity to gain market share by rewarding your customers with economy of scale. This idea may go completely against your grain, but think about the goodwill it could create, especially if you believe you're a customer-driven business. Put yourself in your customer's place and see how that idea feels.

The statement, "When business gets bad, we have to raise the price," could be particularly useful as a way to "zag" when your competition "zigs." For example, bankers

continue to insist on cutting loan rates when
business gets bad. Yet, year after year The
American Banker magazine survey on
issues shows loan rates to be one of the least
important issues to consumers, falling light
years behind service. So if you're a banker,
put what it would cost you to cut loan rates
into a new or improved service.

Finally, the statement, "when business gets
bad we have to cut the inventory," could be
very useful in preventing price cutting. Pay
a lot of attention to business cycles. When
lead indicators show a drop in your
business, run lean.

Then you can sell fewer units at higher
margin and support yourself beautifully
without cutting prices.

"How can these be new ideas?" you ask. "I
already know them." Of course you do.
That's the beauty of the process. You already
have all the answers in you. This just puts
you in a place where you can:

1) See them.

2) Act on them.

IN EVERY PROBLEM YOU CAN FIND THE SEEDS OF ITS OWN SOLUTION.

This means the place to begin to look is at our own habits. To look at all the things we've accepted as being true. Things that we've long since stopped questioning.

So now let's look how this can work for us. Since creativity is the act of creating change, we must understand change before we can fully understand creativity.

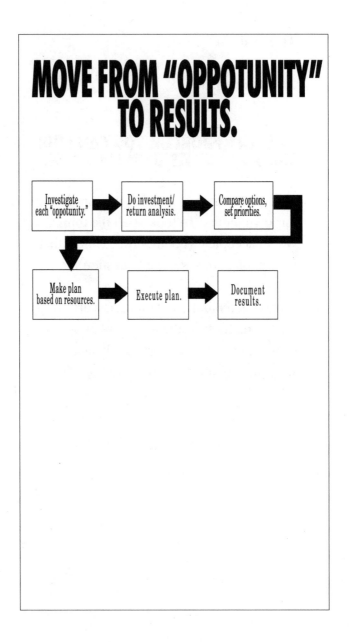

Part IV
INNOVATION THROUGH IMPLEMENTATION.

Chapter Fifteen
THE PRINCIPLE OF UN-CHANGE.

"We are the echo of the future."
– W.S. Merwin

Combine continuous improvement with technology as we have in the 90's, and you have not only change but rapidly accelerating change. Unfortunately, technology also creates expectations. A few years ago, you could ship something and get it there in days. Then, Federal Express innovated with a brilliant distribution opportunity (ship everything to Memphis, then trade packages) and the sophisticated technology of a computer tracking system that cut the time to absolutely positively overnight. Did this innovation relieve stress by creating more time to do things? NO. Rather, it created just the opposite. It created the expectation that people could handle more things in shorter time.

Then, electronics companies innovated with a brilliant communication opportunity (send

your paper over the phone via fax
machines) and the microchip technology
that cut the price to affordable levels. Did
this innovation relieve stress by creating
more time to do things? NO. It also created
just the opposite. It created a further
expectation that people could handle more
things in even shorter time.

So, the paradox: The things that are
supposed to remove the stress from our
lives are often the things that actually
add stress.

And the more things change, the more they
create these expectations. The expectations
are based on our history, but the changes
don't seem to obey our history anymore. So
the expectations prove false when the
results are in. (Convenience devices created
more stress.) And yet our history says that
can't be true. So we don't accept it as true.
And the contradiction between the results
and the history causes even more stress.

Yet, don't just limit this paradox to
convenience devices and technology. It's

virtually everywhere you look, if you have
the eyes to see it. It's in your work. You
now have to do things better. You'd expect
to have more time and more money to
accomplish them. Yet, in many cases you
actually have less time and less money.
How can you be effective working in this
contradiction to your history?

George Ainsworth Land, in his book, *Grow
Or Die,* describes the stages of a company's
change as Formative, Normative and what
others have called Dormative (the decline
stage when the company goes to sleep.)

Land also prescribes an alternate third step
to decline, one that allows a company to
continually regenerate or reinvent itself. It is
by accomplishing this regeneration that
companies are winning today.

In every case, the same theme prevails. To
continually regenerate means that every
person must use new thinking to overcome
their history and as a result their
expectations. The only thing that's been
missing is how.

That's why you have this book in your hands.

CHANGE AND STRESS.

Why does change cause us all so much stress? Think of change as a train pulling out of the station. While you're on the train, you feel a part of what's going on around you. You feel safe and secure. You accept it, it accepts you.

But let's say you jump off the train to get a candy bar, and by the time you return the train has already left. When you watch the train move away into the distance, getting smaller and smaller, what happens to your level of stress?

This is the exact same thing that happens to people when they're faced with significant amounts of change. First, they're part of what's going on. They feel safe and secure. Then, suddenly, "what's going on" leaves them standing at the station.

FAHDEN'S THEORY OF CHANGE AND STRESS: STRESS INCREASES IN DIRECT PROPORTION TO YOUR DISTANCE FROM WHAT'S GOING ON.

If you feel as though you are being left at the station (and you should with the rate of change accelerating daily,) you have several choices.

OPTION ONE (HIGH STRESS:) STAY AT THE STATION.

Many people have chosen this alternative. It's based on what babies do when they're frightened. Sometimes they don't even cry. As said before, they always hang on tight. This option will only work if you are very patient. Over a long period of time what has changed away from you will probably change back to you in one form or another. (As we have established when we covered cyclical change.) But you may be in discomfort for a long time.

OPTION TWO (HIGH STRESS:) STAY ON THE TRAIN.

Some people have chosen this alternative.
It's based on keeping the shortest possible
distance between you and what's going on.
It requires extreme flexibility, even the
willingness to abandon many of your
beliefs. "It changed? I'm going with it."
And while the train is in the station, you
dare not get off to get a candy bar for fear
the train will leave you. You may be in a
different kind of discomfort here. Sort of an
eternal vigilance to make sure you're
always with what's going on.

OPTION THREE (LOW STRESS:) KNOW WHERE THE TRAIN IS GOING, AND TAKE A CAB.

A few people have chosen this alternative. It
means you must keep up on where "what's
going on" is going. You can do this by
reading authors like Alvin Toffler (*Future
Shock, PowerShift,*) Tom Peters (*Thriving
on Chaos*) and others for the forces that
shape our world and what their probable

effects will be. Use that information as your power. Once you understand where the train is going, you can always jump off for a candy bar and catch up with it later.

OPTION FOUR (LOW STRESS:) LAY NEW TRACK.

Fewer people still have chosen this alternative. It's the "build a station and it will come" option. Here, you live out of your own vision and shape your world to fit. Whenever things change away from you, adopt the parts that fit your vision, discard the parts that don't. This will keep you near the train if you choose to be, or up in front guiding the direction. To form your own vision see the chapter on knowing what you want, then use opposites of what you don't want to further your vision of what you do want. Then use the chapter on selling your ideas to get other trains to use the tracks you lay. After all, when you own the railroad, no trains are going to get too far away.

THE PRINCIPLE OF UN-CHANGE.

Many people fear change. One reason is the mistaken belief things will stay the new way and that the old way will be lost forever.

Nothing could be further from the truth. As we've established, most change is cyclical.

So if you're afraid of losing something from change, don't worry. Sooner or later it will change back. If you loved the 1950's, you got them back in many ways in the 1980's. If you loved the 1960's, here they are in some ways in the 90's.

Things always come back to where they started. It's just that they usually do it in a different way.

But there's another way to look at change. One that may make it easier to understand.

Something develops a certain amount of popularity, but it can go only so far without a backlash. At that point it yields to its opposite, or you might say, change yields to un-change.

If you look at history, this happens time and time again in just about every field.

THE RISE AND FALL OF POLYESTER.

Do you know the first time that polyester showed up successfully in consumer products? No-Iron shirts. "Just think," said the advertising, "you'll never have to iron another shirt." So polyester arrived, and it was good. But remember un-change. When something begins to get popular, it's also sowing the seeds of its own downfall. Yet, because consumers accepted polyester, marketers were eager to sell more.

So, next came double-knit slacks. Complete with the crease that wouldn't die. And as you walked and your legs rubbed together. If your petroleum-based pants didn't start an oil-well fire, you could at least depend on picking little balls of fabric off your pants at the most embarrassing times.

No matter, these small inconveniences. Polyester continued its increase in popularity. In fact, enough people bought double knits the fashion industry came up with its piece-de-resistance, the Leisure Suit.

There must have been one night when all the men who bought leisure suits showed up wearing them. It was a Friday night in the mid-70's. Imagine a dance where hundreds of couples enter the room with all the men wearing brand new leisure suits.

For those of you who don't remember, the leisure suit used a heavyweight shirt for a suit coat. The shirt which matched the pants was worn with its tails on the outside, not tucked into the pants. Under the heavy shirt was a brightly contrasting inner shirt made of shiny fabric (polyester, of course,) with a huge pointy collar.

But what made the leisure suit so special was the relationship between these two shirts. That's because you would roll up the sleeves of the inner shirt and the outer shirt at the same time, so that the bright accent of the inner shirt's rolled cuffs would cover the outer shirt. A splendid effect. Then, to

finalize the accent, you'd pull up the collar
of the inner shirt, and fold it back down
again over the outer shirt, guaranteeing
yourself a nifty look.

THE SECRET OF UN-CHANGE. THE LEISURE SUIT WAS SO POPULAR, IT CREATED THE POPULARITY OF ITS OWN OPPOSITE.

Remember the next clothing trend that
swept the nation? The exact opposite.
Artificial yielded to natural. Trendy yielded
to basic. And the preppie look was born.

POPULARITY: IT'S JUST "POLARITY" WITHOUT THE P.U.

For the first time in history, a look that had
quietly existed unchanged for years was
suddenly popularized. What comes in must
go out. What goes up must come down.

Yet, for a short time, the usually stable
cycles of men's fashion hit a huge cycle of

change. And then right after it, hit a huge cycle of un-change.

THE PEOPLE WHO MAKE THE CHANGE KEEP THE CHANGE.

If you are the creator of the change, then you don't have to be its blind effect anymore. Instead, you can plan the change and have it benefit you. That's the advantage of being the creator rather than the observer. Unfortunately, most people don't know how to make change. Yes, we've tried it. Sometimes we've failed and sometimes we've succeeded. But in either case, we haven't known exactly why we've failed or succeeded. Which keeps verifying for our clinging minds that change is still an unknown and scary process.

And well it should be, because most people don't even have a process for change.

Chapter Sixteen
LEARNING TO LOVE CONTRADICTIONS.

"In the Highlands of New Guinea I saw men with photographs of themselves mounted on their foreheads, so they would be recognized."
– Ted Carpenter

In 1963 America noticed four strange-looking British youths. They were a group called the Beatles.
What was it about them that caught so much attention? Let's explore that from the viewpoint of your own newly re-emerging creativity.

For one thing, they created visual opposites. Perhaps the most radical was their hair. American men had short hair for several generations. Yet those four Brits had long hair. At the time to the short-haired Americans, long hair on men meant either of two things: You are a rebel or a woman.

But the Beatles added yet another contradiction with their music. Here they created even more powerful visual/verbal opposites.

If you thought they looked like rebels, then why was their music so innocent? ("I Wanna Hold Your Hand.")

If you thought they were men trying to look like women, why was their music so clearly heterosexual?

To make matters even more contrary to the visual opposite of long hair, they had good manners, were well-dressed, neatly groomed and clean. In fact their Edwardian suits helped resolve the opposite of their hair by taking the viewer back to a time when longer hair was actually worn with those suits. So the opposite can incorporate its way into real change when the viewer has a way to resolve the opposite, to make sense of it based on something that is either acceptable now, or has been acceptable at one time.

THE COMPUTER MIND.

As we have established, the mind cannot stand a contradiction (Two opposites in one thought.) So the mind will not rest until that contradiction is resolved, one way or the other. (This is why you chose "stove-hot" and forgot about the possibilities of "stove-cold.")

The Beatles created a visual picture of males opposite the one that existed in our culture. Had their music not been so innocent, they would have simply confirmed beliefs that already existed about long hair, and therefore, they would have moved no one.

ATTENTION: THE FIRST STEP IN CHANGE.

Looking more closely, the Beatles accomplished the first thing you need when you're creating change: attention.

The Advertising Textbooks suggest creating change in buyers' habits this way:

ATTENTION, INTEREST, DECISION,
ACTION– (AIDA.) To change behavior,
you must have all four. After all, without
attention, how can you get someone's
interest? And without their interest, how can
you get them to make a decision? And
so on.

The Beatles created attention masterfully by
showing themselves as visual opposites to
our culture's most basic and obvious pictures.

Then they commanded interest by creating
music that was extremely opposite what
you'd expect from their visual picture.

The decision and action come in the usual
ways. The early adopters made it safe for
everyone to like these "strange" youths
from England.

But this decision and action never would
have happened had the Beatles not used
such extreme opposites to capture the
attention and interest in the first place.

Chapter Seventeen
HOW TO KNOW WHEN YOU'VE GONE TOO FAR.

*"If you have any notion of where
you are going, you will never
get anywhere."*
– Joan Kro

What if the Beatles would have shown up in long hair and black leather jackets? Actually, that's what they wore before they were successful. But people interpreted black leather jackets into their prior beliefs about rebels and motorcycle gangs. So the opposites went too far in one direction to be original.

There is a way for you to know whether the opposites you create are too far from cultural norms for people to accept.

The first way: Know how you can fail. There are two basic ways you can go too far in creating opposites.

1. Errors of clarity.
2. Errors of taste.

ERRORS OF CLARITY.

In any communication you can operate with
the principle of Gestalt. Loosely translated,
it means the less information the mind
receives, the more it wants to participate.

Remember the "Mary" story? "Mary heard
the bell. With birthday money in hand,
Mary ran down the stairs."

Remember your original interpretation of
the story.

Did she live in an old white wood frame
house or a modern one? Was she wearing a
party dress or jeans? Was the bell an ice
cream truck, or was she at school and it was
a fire alarm?

Now read it again and see if what you saw
was really there, or if your mind filled in the
blanks from your own experience.

You've just experienced the principle of
Gestalt at work: If you want to increase
involvement, decrease information.

Yet therein lies the danger, as well. (Every opportunity contains the seeds of its own destruction, just as every disaster contains the seeds of opportunity.) Gestalt works well up to a point. After that, you've decreased information beyond understanding, and then you've lost your viewer.

For example, if you go opposite a style that's literal and, therefore, fills in all the information, be sure you give the viewers enough stimulus to use as a framework for their information. Then you have a powerful Gestalt working for you.

How do you know what that critical point is? Simple. Just show your concept to someone who doesn't care. Ask them to tell you what it means. Either they get it or they don't. If they don't, add more information bit by bit until they do.

If they do get it, ask if it's powerful. If it's not, take out some information and then show it to someone else, and see if they get it. Eventually, you'll hit just the right amount for the optimum Gestalt.

ERRORS OF TASTE.

You'll find that this one may be just a little more tricky. Jerry Della Femina, author of *From Those Wonderful Folks Who Gave You Pearl Harbor*, says that the best advertising borders on bad taste.

The key here is which side of the border you're on. We've all suppressed a darker side of our nature that lures us into humor and other rebellion against "good taste."

But once the opposite crosses certain lines, it offends rather than tickles. And, of course, the context dictates much about where this line is.

Tell an off-color joke in a sports bar and you'll create one effect. Tell the same joke from the pulpit in church, and you may cross some of those lines.

That's because the idea tends to overpower the beliefs and values that are already in the person, so the mind rebels. Just as the body shuts down when physical trauma causes overload, so does the mind when mental trauma causes overload.

So again, the best way to see if your idea has gone over the line on taste issues is to show it to people. But this time, show it to people in different contexts as well. The lines of taste are not as universal as the lines of clarity. You may want to sacrifice a little more of your power, and turn down the bad taste two or three extra notches. That way you run less risk of losing part of your audience.

Chapter Eighteen
HOW TO CHOOSE THE BEST IDEAS.

"It gets late early here."
– Yogi Berra

Once you have some powerful concepts, you need some basis from which to select the ones that will work best for you.

Naturally, you'll already have some of your own selection criteria, even if it's simply: I like this one, I don't like that. Or in many cases: The boss will like this one; The boss won't like that.

Further, you can group your ideas into four basic categories.

UBIQUITY: From the word "ubiquitous." Being everywhere at once. (Ideas you've already seen a lot.)

UNIQUITY: It's powerfully unique.

UNITY: The two opposite elements also fit together due to some obvious similarities.

UTILITY: The new combination offers some useful benefits.

For example, if you're entering a market that's filled with communications, you may wish to select an idea that has powerful UNIQUITY so that you can get above the noise.

Or if you see a need for practical innovation, go for utility.

HOW MUCH MONEY SHOULD YOU CARRY IN YOUR SHOES?

Imagine a pair of traditional "penny" loafers. How much money would you normally carry in them?
If you were going for UBIQUITY (ideas you've already seen a lot), you'd obviously carry two cents, a penny in each loafer. Now what about UNIQUITY? (It's powerfully unique.) What's the most extreme opposite of a penny? Well, if you're dealing in U.S. currency, it's a $100,000 bill in each shoe. It would get you

a lot of attention, but it's not very easy to cash and would obviously be dangerous to carry (potential theft).

Now try UNITY. (The two opposite elements, fit together due to some obvious similarities.) Think about which other U.S. currency is similar yet opposite to the penny. Opposite: A bill is opposite a coin. Similar: How about Lincoln? He's on both the penny and the five-dollar bill. What's more, if you fold the five-dollar bill just right, the oval frame around the president's head will peek out of your shoe in roughly the same size and shape as the coin.

Then, we can't forget UTILITY. (The new combination offers some useful benefits.) How about a fifty-dollar bill in each shoe? Imagine forgetting your wallet on your way out to dinner with a bunch of strangers. It could be embarrassing to have to ask a stranger for money. Until you remember: "Ahhh. I've got $100 in my shoes."

Chapter Nineteen
INNOVATION ON DEMAND FOR MARKETING COMMUNICATIONS.

"If you think you're free, there's no escape possible."
– Ram Dass

If you want to cut an enormous amount of the time it takes to do the concept work for any marketing communications campaign, apply the Innovation on Demand method.

Not only can you use this concept for achieving immediate results, but it will give you a much better chance of getting others to agree with the work you've done.

START WITH THE VON RESTORFF EFFECT.

Von Restorff discovered a very helpful principle when he conducted research on how we get our information. He first confirmed we perceive elements in a sequence, no matter what source we use. For example, if we read a magazine, we turn

the pages one after another. If we watch TV,
the commercials don't come on all at the
same time; they come on one after another.
The same is true for radio, outdoor
advertising, direct mail and any other
advertising media.

So, Von Restorff measured perception and
discovered two major principles:

1. If in any sequence, all elements are pretty
much the same, the best remembered will be
the first and the last. (Maybe this is why the
magazines charge advertisers a premium for
the back cover and the inside front and
back pages.)

THE VON
RESTORFF EFFECT.

XXXXXXXXXXXXXXXXX

This principle won't do you much good,
except maybe to give you a warm feeling
when you pay the preferred advertising
space charges.

2. If any element significantly breaks the
pattern, it will be remembered far in excess
of either the first or the last elements.

THE VON RESTORFF EFFECT.

XXXXXXXXXOXXXXXXX

This principle will do you a lot of good,
because it's about the only leverage left in
the advertising process. (Define leverage
here as the ability to get a larger value or
greater result than the amount of dollars
you've paid.)

Perhaps this is why David Ogilvy, in his
book, *Confessions of an Advertising Man,*

states you can increase the response to an advertisement by a multiple of 10 to 1 simply by changing the headline.

And perhaps this is why the difference between one of the best-testing commercials of all time (Volkswagen, 91) and one of the-worst testing commercials of all time (Chevrolet, 6) yielded a leverage of about 15 to 1. In other words, had all other things been equal, VW would have outsold Chevrolet by 15 to 1. In fact, at the time (the early 1960's) the VW "Bug" came out of nowhere to become the first import to be the number two model of car in the U.S. simply by the effectiveness of its advertising.

Consider this: In 1959, it was obvious that "Americans will buy only big cars." And the bigger the better. The 1959 Cadillac was 20 feet long, and sported tail fins that could impale you if you got too close. Not a very hopeful picture for Volkswagen who had a small car — a very small car. Yet by 1965, the VW Bug was the second largest selling model automobile in the U. S., just behind Chevrolet's Impala. What happened?

THE TIME TO BE HOPEFUL IS WHEN THINGS LOOK HOPELESS.

What happened was a shift, actually several shifts,created by a talented advertising team who could read the cycles, play off the obvious and change the minds of American consumers.

The team, art directors George Lois and Helmut Krone and copywriter Julian Koenig, were assigned by their agency, Doyle, Dane, Bernbach, to develop the soon-to-be landmark VW campaign. This team saw that there was already a small group of people who liked the car.

These were people who appreciated the car's engineering and simplicity (which, along with the car's smallness, was also not obvious in 1959).

The team saw its goal, then, as expanding the size of that group. But how to do it? Lois and his collaborators decided first that to be successful in the U.S. they needed to sell a lot of VWs in New York. ("The problem," wrote George Lois in his book, *George, Be Careful*, was how a Greek art director could sell a Nazi car in a Jewish town.)

VW's ads didn't scream. But by presenting themselves, and their product, in a completely opposite way, they stood out. In effect, they got above the noise by creating a completely different tone.

HOW TO BREAK THE PATTERN SUCCESSFULLY.

Simple. Go to the opposite. But first you must clearly recognize what the pattern is. The people who worked on the Volkswagen advertising first looked at the context of the product.

AMERICA LOVES BIG CARS.

Then they went to the opposite.

AMERICA LOVES SMALL CARS.

They also looked at the context of
advertising for cars at the time.

CAR ADVERTISING IS FULL OF HYPE.

Then they went to the opposite.

CAR ADVERTISING IS BRUTALLY HONEST.

Each of these opposites may sound like a
huge contradiction until you ask. "How
could this be true?"

How could "AMERICA LOVES SMALL
CARS" be true? First, think about
Newton's first law of motion: for every
action there is an equal and opposite
reaction. Because most change is cyclical,
there will always be a group of people, no
matter how small, who believe this opposite
as though it were already true. In VW's
case, they looked at who had already bought
the car.

So if you're advertising a product, look first at the people who have already bought it, your USERS. They will tell you exactly what needs your product fills for them and open the doorway to attracting more people just like them.

In the case of Volkswagen, they found an independent thinker who loved the simplicity of the "Bug." This, then, was Volkswagen's cue. Find more people just like that by advertising to them in a memorable way.

WHERE TO LOOK FOR YOUR OWN OPPOSITES.

1. Product or Service. Look for a place where all the competitive products cluster. (Big cars: VW became the opposite. Slow delivery services: Federal Express became the opposite. Left-brain computers: Apple became the opposite.) Usually you'll find the biggest "oppotunity" in the most obvious beliefs about the product or service category. Then, simply, go to the opposite.

2. Marketing. Look for the most obvious ways in which the product or service is delivered, where all the competitors tend to cluster. (Car customer pays for service: Audi became the opposite with the free service of "three-year test drive.")

3. Creative. Look for the most obvious ways in which the product or service is advertised, where the competitors tend to cluster. (Advertisers run their own commercials: The Energizer Bunny became the opposite with its walk through other (faked) commercials).

PUT THE COMPETITORS UP AGAINST THE WALL WITH "OPPOSCALES."

Tear out all your competitor's print ads and tape them to the wall. You're going to rate each one on seven scales of opposites. Look for the scales where the competitors all show up on one end.

Count the total number of ads.

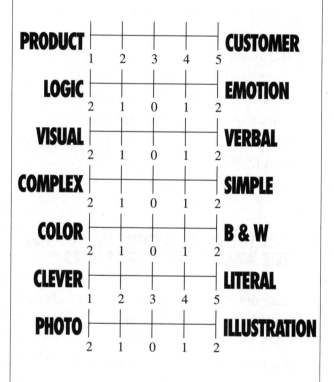

1. Count Product-Focused vs. Customer-Focused ads. How many of the ads speak directly about the product? Or, how many speak to the customer's need that drives them to want the product?

2. Count Logic vs. Emotion ads. How many of the ads speak directly to the logic of the reader? And how many speak directly to the emotion of the reader? You'll be surprised how many are logic-based because that's the way business people are expected to think.

3. Count Visual vs. Verbal ads. Which dominates each ad? Is it a huge headline, or dominant visual with a small headline?

4. Count Complex vs. Simple ads.

5. Count Color vs. Black and White ads.

6. Count Clever vs. Literal ads.

7. Count Photography vs. Illustration ads.

The larger the ratio of one opposite to the other, the bigger your "oppotunity." Let's say you have 20 ads.

The score 20-0, Logical. A big opportunity
to do emotional ads.

The score 18-2, Product-Focused. A big
opportunity to do Customer-Focused ads.

The score 12-8, Verbal. Not so big of
an opportunity.

In this case you may want to leave it alone
and use the opposite where you've caught
the competition leaning in the other
direction. Then use the principles of martial
arts and give your competition a little shove
in the direction they were already going.

Use the same process to create agreement
on your direction.

Once you've created your ads as opposites
to the obvious (in this case *emotional,
reader focused* ads,) take anyone you need
to agree with you through this same process.
Once they see it step-by-step, it will be very
difficult for them to disagree, unless they
have some information that you don't. And
in that case, you can make a mid-course
correction and everyone will win.

Use a process that helped the Allies win
World War II.

Rather than attacking Europe head on, they
first fought their way up through Italy, the
soft underbelly of the continent. The
opposite of the expected.

You can do the same in establishing your
ideal outcome.

It's called the issues grid, and it will tell you
what actions to take.

ISSUES GRID

WHAT ARE YOUR TOP PRIORITIES? If this were to turn out absolutely ideal, what needs would have been met?	HOW IMPORTANT IS EACH? KEY: + = Very Important 0 = So, So - = Not Important	HOW GOOD ARE WE AT EACH? KEY: + = Very Good 0 = So, So - = Not Good	Competitors		
			A	B	C

HOW TO USE YOUR CREATIVITY TO WIN WITH OTHERS.

If you're going to accomplish anything, you need the support of other people.

If you're selling, you need others to buy.

If you're performing, you need an audience.

If you're working, you need others to approve your work.

To help you in this, a concept you may want to adopt is that of the "internal customer."

This idea expands the concept of "customer" to mean: Anyone that you agree to do anything for.

If you agree to submit a report to your boss, then until the report is approved, the boss is the customer.

Here is a system to find out exactly what your customers want, so you can present what you're offering in a way they will want it.

Or, as the old saying goes, the difference between selling and marketing is this:

"Selling is 1/4 inch drills."

"Marketing is 1/4 inch holes."

In other words, to you, it's a drill with a variable speed feature and a 3/8 inch chuck and a 1/4 inch bit.

To the customer, it's the need to put a hole in the wall with smooth edges and minimum mess.

1. IMPORTANCE. THE IDEAL OUTCOME FOR YOUR CUSTOMER.

This dimension will allow you to set priorities in your work. Then once you know what's important, add the dimension of performance so you'll know what to do next.

2. PERFORMANCE. YOUR CUSTOMER'S PERCEPTION OF HOW WELL YOU DO ON THE IMPORTANT ISSUES.

Now see how well you perform on each issue. If you perform well on an important issue, take credit for it. If you don't perform well, protect your flank by improving your performance on it. Ultimately, you will perform well on every important issue, thus assuring yourself a bright future.

HOW TO MOVE AHEAD OF COMPETITORS.

Often, others are trying to get the same things you want. In business, it can be your direct competitors.

In the office, it can be someone who needs the share of budget you need for your project.

Just like the concept of internal customer, a competitor is anyone who wants the same thing you do, if the supply is limited.

Use the important-issues grid as a way to move ahead of your competitors. When you learn the customer's perception of how you perform on important issues, also learn the customer's perception of how your competitors perform on important issues.

THE IDEAL STRATEGY.

Your ideal strategy should be based on an important issue where your performance is strong and your leading competitor's performance is weak. Then you'll be attacking the "weak underbelly of Europe."

Follow these five steps and you'll win more often than not:

1. Know why you're doing this. (*"If the why is big enough, the how is no problem."*) -Nietzsche.

A. It's the one system that allows you to attack a competitor's weak point.

B. It also allows you to put priority to your work on the basis of what's important to your customer. You gain valuable time by not having to do the unimportant work.

2. Get the following information from your customer:

A. If they were to have the ideal of your product or service, how would they describe it? What they describe as the ideal's characteristics are the most important issues.

B. Have them rate those issues from top to bottom. (+ is very important, 0 is so-so and - is not important).

C. If the needs from the top issues were not met, what problems would it cause?

D. If these problems existed, what emotions would it bring up? (Emotions drive behavior, and that's what you want in the first place.)

3. Get your customer's perception on how well you and your competitors perform on these important issues.

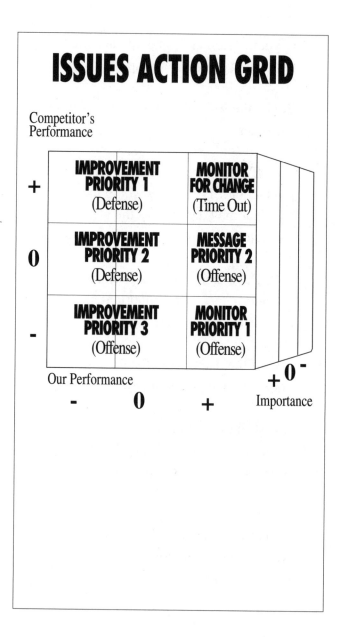

A. Perception is reality. It doesn't matter how well you think you perform; just what your customer thinks.

B. Use a three-point scale. (+ is very good, 0 is so-so and - is not good.)

4. Draw up your Issues List.

A. List the issues on the left and put two columns on the right, one for importance and one each for how well you and your competitors perform.

B. Note the important issues where you are + and your competitors are 0 or -. This, then, is the key issue for your advertising strategy.

5. Transfer the information to the Issues Action Grid. This will give you a clear picture of what to do with the information.

A. Put the important issues on which you perform well in the upper right corner. Those that capitalize on a competitor's weakness (choose the one with the largest market share) should be your primary focus in advertising. The others in this quadrant should be your secondary advertising copy points.

B. Put the important issues on which you don't perform well in the upper left corner. These issues should direct your work plan for improvement.

This process improvement should be done as soon as possible because poor performance on these important issues make you vulnerable to competitors.

C. Put the unimportant issues in the lower two corners. For now, do nothing with them. You save time by not doing unnecessary work. Use this time savings to fund the time you put into improving the important issues you don't perform well on. This will protect your flanks in the short term, and move you ahead of your competition in the long run with continuous improvement.

Now you have the basis for the ideal strategy.

Chapter Twenty
HOW TO CONVINCE OTHERS YOUR IDEAS ARE GOOD.

"It doesn't matter if the water is cold or warm if you're going to have to wade through it anyway."
— Teilhard de Chardin

Use opposites to sell your ideas. You can win in two different ways by doing this.

1. You can go opposite conventional selling wisdom and outperform the best sales people.

2. You can present your ideas in the opposite direction so that the other person arrives at the same conclusions.

HOW TO GO OPPOSITE CONVENTIONAL SELLING WISDOM AND WIN.

In the book, *S.P.I.N. Selling* by Neil Rakham, he surprised himself and all the clients who had asked him to make ways of

"closing" a sale more sophisticated.
Ironically, after studying more than 35,000
sales calls, he found the opposite to be true:
That closing the sale was not helpful, except
in sales of small ticket items. In larger
purchases, a "closer" (one who was
persistent about asking for the order)
actually irritated the customers.

What did work was the opposite of focusing
on the end of the sale. That was focusing
on the work done at the beginning of the
sale. The more of that accomplished (such
as establishing the customer's needs,) the
higher the performance on the sale.

HOW TO GO IN THE OPPOSITE DIRECTION AND WIN.

The obvious belief is that to get your way,
you must win others over to your point of
view. The powerful opposite: you must win
others over to their point of view.

Think of persuasion as a river. You stand on
one bank with your new idea. The other

person stands on the other bank, set in their old ideas.

You must build a bridge across that river. Only then will you make it easy for the two for you to get together on your new idea.

Most bridge builders make one fatal mistake. They build the bridge from the wrong side. Which side should you build your bridge from?

The obvious side: your side.

The opposite side: their side.

How can the opposite side be true? Look at it from the metaphor of the bridge. If you build the bridge from your side (meaning, start the presentation with your idea, and then give all the reasons why it's a good idea,) no matter how far you build the bridge towards them, it's still on your side of the river. They can't even take step one toward you without getting wet. So until you finish the entire presentation, they can make no moves at all toward agreeing with you. So your presentation will merely reinforce the habit they're already in.

Now look at the opposite. Build your bridge beginning with their side. Now with every span you build, they get closer and closer to you. So you are actually bringing them across the river to your point of view.
How do you do this? You can go opposite conventional selling wisdom and outperform the best sales people.

In other words, you can begin to build the bridge from the other side by investigating what the other person has for needs and wants and what options they have to meet them. Then, you can build more spans of the bridge by relating different aspects of your idea to helping them get what they want. Finally you can reveal your idea and how accomplishing it is the best alternative for them.

For example, let's say your idea is to sell refrigerators to Eskimos as a way to keep their food from freezing, and you're speaking to the head of refrigerator marketing.

Begin to build the bridge from the other side by investigating what the other person needs and wants in the general area of refrigerator sales. Then, build more spans of the bridge by relating different aspects of your idea to helping them get more refrigerators sales.

"You know John, we've never cracked the Eskimo market, and there are thousands of them without refrigerators. What if we could find a way where they needed one?"

Finally you can reveal the "keep their food from freezing" idea and how accomplishing it is the best alternative for them.

"We've done some new thinking on this that could get some results we've never had. It will take a big shift in all of our thinking to do it, but once we think that way, it could be fast and easy to sell a lot of refrigerators. Are you willing to make a big thinking leap with me for a few minutes?"

Notice that every step of the way John gets
an opportunity to decide what's in it for him
before he takes another step across the
bridge. There are no big missing spans in
the bridge, nowhere for him to fall in the
water. This is a safe bridge. All it takes is
your willingness to swim over to his side
before you start building.

What if the reason is: "I don't have enough
money."

The opposite: "I have too much money."
How could this be true?

1. Everyone spends money that doesn't help
them get what they want. The spending
may be started with good intentions, but
often the promise of value stops and the
spending goes on by virtue of habit.

Think of all the business vendors people
continue to use, even though their
performance is marginal. The relationships
continue for many reasons:

"I don't want to upset people."

"It's too hard to find someone better."

"If I find someone better, they may turn out to be worse."

So the habits go on tying up the funds that could finance what you want them to do.

2. Another way, they could have "too much money:" Ask them to recall a time when they've had to get rid of money. It might have been spending a budget to be sure it was renewed for the next year.

Or it might have been pre-paying invoices to get them into a calendar year to wipe out a tax liability. Or it might have been spending a budget item they knew they weren't going to use for something else on products or services that would contribute more value. For example, spending the unused portion of a travel and entertainment budget on training.

The point is, when you realize the ways you have too much money, there's always enough.

Then you repeat: "I have too much time."
And then ask "How could this be true?"

This gives the other person an "oppotunity"
to discover a new way of thinking about his
or her directions.

How could it be true that a busy person has
too much time?

1. If people are very busy, chances are
they're not managing their time well. So ask
them to think of the non-productive time
they spent during the last week. It may help
to define non-productive time as time spent
not accomplishing what you want, (i.e.
fighting fires, taking care of complainers,
etc.)

2. Ask them to look at their calendar 30 to
60 days in the future. Chances are it's
almost blank. That's where they have too
much time. So have them plan with you that
far in advance.

WHAT TO DO IF SOMEONE STILL DOESN'T SEE THINGS YOUR WAY.

When someone gives you a specific reason they don't want to do as you ask, you encounter a third persuasion opportunity, the brief opposite.

The moment they give you the reason, acknowledge that it's an important one.

Then ask if they'd be willing to look at it another way. If they say "yes" (and they usually do,) ask them to look at the opposite of their reason and see how it could be true.

For example, one other frequent reason is: It's not a priority. So, present the following:

The obvious, other priorities are great.

The opposite, other priorities are small. How could this be true? One possibility. If that other priority is so great, why haven't you done it?

Chapter Twenty One
THE DEEPER INNOVATION ON DEMAND.

"Don't solve the problem, just give it up."
– Author Unknown

Use the following pages as a way to get deeper into Innovation On Demand.

If you're stuck, look at the list of frequent mistakes for each step of the method "Where People Most Often Get Stuck." Acknowledge mistakes are normal and a way to learn, then go for it again.

After all, it took Edison almost 1000 tries before he got the light bulb he wanted.

Use Innovation On Demand and you'll get there faster.

THE OUTCOME: WHERE PEOPLE MOST OFTEN GET STUCK.

1. NOT KNOWING WHAT YOU WANT.
Avoid this by focusing on something that

will create value for either you or your customer.

2. CHOOSING AN OUTCOME THAT'S NO DIFFERENT FROM WHAT YOU HAVE. Beware of statements that start out with "Do a better job of..." Instead, go for the most difficult outcome, because you now have the method to accomplish it.

THE OBVIOUS: WHERE PEOPLE MOST OFTEN GET STUCK.

1. USING WORD ASSOCIATIONS THAT AREN'T OBVIOUS ENOUGH. Almost everyone agrees with what's obvious about Eskimos because so few people actually know one. Yet, that's not necessarily true about grocery check-out people. So you may have to look a little harder to find something obvious about them.

Always go to the most basic associations. (Grocery check-out people run cash registers.) Avoid those that may not be as consistent. (Grocery check-out people are Republicans.)

2. FORGETTING TO PUT THE
OBVIOUS WORDS INTO A SENTENCE.
There's no point in doing opposites if you
can't use a full sentence to create a
contradiction. Many people forget this point
and will deal in single words only and
wonder what happened. For example, let's
say one outcome word is "stove" and you
write down "hot" as your first obvious
association. In the next step, when you write
down "cold" as the opposite, it will do you
no good unless you connect "cold" back to
"stove."

So, always put your obvious word into a
sentence that relates it to the association
"Stoves are hot." Then you can create a
contradiction like: "Stoves are cold."

Just remember this: Obvious: Create the
most obvious association. Then put each in
a sentence.

THE OPPOSITE: WHERE PEOPLE MOST OFTEN GET STUCK.

1. LIMITING THE POTENTIAL BY THINKING THAT WORDS HAVE ONLY ONE OPPOSITE. If you want to uncover more Opposites, go back to the Obvious word and change the meaning. For example, "cold" can be limiting if you take it only to mean temperature. Yet, it can also mean "unfriendly."

This means you can extend your "oppotunity" by adding "friendly" to the list of opposites of "cold."

2. FAILING TO RECOGNIZE SHADES OF MEANING. You can also use "warm" as an Opposite of "cold." In other words, your opposite doesn't have to be "hot," a polar opposite to be useful. One helpful technique is to work your way back from a polar opposite to the center until something spurs a practical solution. For example, "refrigerators keep food hot" means you can keep a delivered pizza hot. "Refrigerators keep food warm" can mean you'll keep your food from freezing. Opposite: Create a contradiction and ask "How could this be true?"

THE "OPPOTUNITY": WHERE PEOPLE MOST OFTEN GET STUCK.

1. If your "oppotunity" isn't powerful enough, or if it yields a solution you've already seen before, go to the Opposite of the other word in the Obvious sentence (your original "Outcome" word.)

For example, let's say your Obvious statement is "Pants are worn by fathers." The Opposite, then, is "Pants are worn by mothers." So what? Women have been wearing pants for decades.

So then, try this: GO TO THE OPPOSITE OF THE ORIGINAL "OUTCOME" WORD. In this case keep your obvious sentence, but go to the opposite of the word from your Outcome statement: "Pants are worn by fathers." "Skirts are worn by fathers." Now there's a more contradictory statement. Then say, "How can this be true?

Is it cross-dressing fathers, or possibly
Scottish fathers in kilts?"

2. FAILURE TO DOCUMENT YOUR
RESULTS. When you get good ideas, write
them down. After you write them down,
choose the best and act on them. After you
act on them, keep track of what happened.
After you get success with Innovation On
Demand, don't fall back into your old
habits. Keep using the method. Move from
"OPPOTUNITY" to results.
Tests have shown that non-creative people
can ideate as well as creative people. The
only difference: non-creatives don't believe
it, so they dismiss their own best ideas.
Don't let that happen to you. Keep going.

AFTER DOING EVERYTHING PERFECTLY: WHERE PEOPLE MOST OFTEN GET STUCK.

Even if you're perfect, your problem itself
can get you stuck. Maybe the problem
doesn't demand a dramatic solution, or it
isn't all that difficult to begin with. Or

maybe a dramatic or powerful solution will create more problems than they solve.

So, if you're using the method and not getting the results you want, and you've tried all the ways of getting unstuck, try this.

Do the Opposite of the method. Go for Unity first, Opposites second.

1. Choose the key words in your Outcome statement, and see whether there are any words common to each of the two.

For example, if your Outcome statement is "Sell Seeds to Retailers," what one word would be common to both seeds and retailers? How about "grow?" Seeds grow, retailers want to grow their business. Now find an elegant way to connect these two. It may be verbal unity (grow) or it may be visual unity (plants represented as line graphs.)

2. Then ask yourself how could these meanings be true, then make them more and more opposite as you go. "Seeds go in the

ground/seeds go out the door." The key is
this: Once you've created unity, now you
want to go for power. This gives you true
"OPPOTUNITY," that elegant unity of
opposites.

Part V
SPECIAL SECTIONS.

Qualitivity.
HOW INNOVATION ON DEMAND CAN IMPROVE YOUR PROCESS IMPROVEMENT.

"There's nothing common about common sense."
— Dr. W. Edwards Deming

When your company commits to a quality program, you begin to build the base for survival in the years to come. It is true that the Japanese have a 40-year head start on the principles and methods of Dr. Deming, and they haven't exactly been standing still. And yet, companies like General Electric, Motorola, AT&T, Xerox, IBM and more have found places to use the same methods where they can still excel.

In a 1991 Fortune article, shortly after Xerox used Deming's methods to eliminate $225 million dollars worth of unneeded inventory from their system, the company's CEO stated quality is not enough, and "...we need innovation in every area."

So, in this special section on quality we will accomplish two ends.

1. We will ground you in enough quality principles and methods so that, even if you are not presently doing a program, you will create results for yourself for now and the future.

2. We will show you how to accomplish the next leap in quality improvement: creativity, so that you can go beyond the other people who are doing quality and move into the lead.

THE "QUALITIVITY" MOVEMENT: CREATIVITY IS THE NEXT STEP BEYOND QUALITY.

One hundred years after the Industrial Revolution, management began to wake up to the idea that when something went wrong you could do more than blame people. Edwards Deming led the way with the concept that "94% of failure is system failure," not people failure. The Japanese

embraced the idea and used it to become a
world economic power. And now the gospel
of quality is spreading throughout the
world. The U.S. founded the Malcolm
Baldridge award and then changed the
criteria to 100% Deming principles. Self-
directed teams that continually improve
process have sprung up in companies of all
sizes and kinds. Consultants teach Deming's
methods to all levels of management.

WHEN EVERYONE DOES QUALITY, INNOVATION WILL MAKE THE DIFFERENCE.

How will you create competitive advantage
in the years, even months, to come? Quality
will only catch you up, and you'll have to
move very fast to do that. So why not find
out where the competition is weak, and
bypass them in one leap?

Most improvement teams learn the methods
and follow them blindly, or at least in a
linear fashion. In other words they look at
improvement like a school assignment and

want to "do it right." Your opportunity lies in the opposite.

WHY DO THINGS RIGHT WHEN YOU CAN DO THE RIGHT THING?

Instead of blindly following quality methods, use creativity to improve your process improvement process.

1. Ask the question, "do we really need this process in the first place?"

2. If you're blocked in improving the process, use opposites to come up with a new, more creative way to solve the problem.

For example, Kris N.'s company asked the question: "do we really need this process in the first place?" to save an enormous amount of money and time in the graphic arts area.

They examined their keyline (typesetting and preparation of camera-ready art for printing) process to solve obvious problems and found they could avoid revisions by involving all key players in a review at the laser print stage. This would catch all mistakes before the costlier production stages began.

Kris, however, applied the Innovation On Demand method in this way. The Obvious: Keylines are visible. The Opposite: Keylines are invisible. The answer to the question, "How could this be true?" You can see big boards, but you can't see the contents of a computer diskette. Kris, then, recommended the test of a "boardless" keyline. The client would still see laser prints, but the usual printing, pasting and mounting steps would be eliminated, saving time and money.

HOW DO YOU KNOW WHICH STEPS YOU CAN ELIMINATE?

Use the principle of Pareto, who invented the way to separate the significant few from the insignificant many. In other words the 20-80 rule. (20% of the people create 80% of the sales, 20% of the problems create

80% of the pain, 20% of the action creates
80% of the results.) Kris conceived the most
important steps to her clients were to see
that the keyline looked correct. Once that
was complete, it didn't matter to the client
how it got to the printer. And to the printer,
the diskette was just fine.

HOW DO YOU KNOW WHICH STEPS ARE MOST IMPORTANT TO THE CLIENT?

Ask. Use the issues grid, introduced in
Chapter 15. The issues grid can be used as a
context for all your quality improvement
thinking. In other words, do the things first
that make the biggest difference. This will
create a shorter cycle time for you, and give
you competitive advantage in the time-
sensitive 90's. And the time you save by not
doing the unimportant things can fund the
time for more process improvements, and
then even a shorter work week.

HOW TO UNBLOCK THE PROCESS IMPROVEMENT.

Jeff's company was trying to get rid of a liability in the form of hospitality services that were losing money. They just couldn't get enough volume to make them pay for themselves, and therefore were thought of as "bad" within the company. The Obvious: Services are bad. The Opposite: Services are good. How could this be true?

HOW TO WIN IN YOUR JOB AND CAREER.

The first way to win your job is not to let the usual processes occur. It's like the military camp where dysentery grew to epidemic proportions. They tried everything: boiling the water, giving people medicine and shots, but nothing worked. Until finally, one day, someone came into the camp, looked around, walked out to the adjoining river and said: "Why don't you put the latrines *down river* from the camp?" The camp had been polluting its own drinking water.

DEFINING THE JOB.

While the analogy is perhaps far-fetched, the same thing may be true with you. What you need to do, even before you go to work, is to investigate the needs of those you are working for.

First, let's define who that person is. I am going to define that person as an *internal* customer. An internal customer is someone you agree to do a task for. So, if somebody asks you to get a pencil, the moment you agree to get the pencil, that person is your internal customer.

The next moment, you could ask that person to get you a piece of paper. That makes you the internal customer, the other person, the vendor or supplier. If you deal with all your tasks in this fashion, it can take you into a whole new way of being. That is, how do you serve your customer? Once you define the person who asks you to perform tasks as your customer, it's like owning your own business. The mission of your business is to serve this customer, and do it in the best way possible.

PICK UP THE TOOLS.

So, let's get into some of the tools that will help you serve your internal customer. THE FIRST TOOL IS INVESTIGATION. The ideal investigation outcome is a list of issues. Those issues and considerations can be anything that is important (or not important) to the delivery of your service to this internal customer. (Review chapter 19 for more.)

For example, an important issue may be that you deliver your results promptly. Another important issue may be that you make changes rapidly in your work plans (without being upset at being asked to make these changes). Another issue may be, the final product is neatly bound in presentation form. To one customer, it may be unimportant. Yet, to another customer of yours, this may be an important issue.

USE THE METHOD.

1. The first step in investigating is to get a list of issues from your internal customer.

The best way to do this is to simply ask. For
example, you may say: "If this project were
to turn out ideally for you, what needs
would have been met?" This statement is an
invitation for your internal customer to start
telling you what issues are most important.

Simply make a list of these issues and keep
asking more questions, until you are
satisfied all the important ones have
come out.

Next, show that list to your internal
customer, and ask for a rating on each issue,
(the higher the rating, the more important
the issue.) That way you can find out which
issues are going to be your biggest
priorities. The joy of doing this is not only
knowing which issues are most important,
but also which issues are not important.
This is a way of cutting down your
workload. You can create a lot of extra time
to do well on the important issues by
leaving the unimportant issues alone. A
vital point, because otherwise you would be
setting yourself up for a lot more work.
Now, in reality you are setting yourself up

for *less* work by concentrating on the
important work.

2. The second step: investigate the
consequences of not getting the needs met.
For example, if you did a plan, and the plan
could not be quickly altered, what would be
the consequences? A way to investigate this
is to ask: "What problems would this cause
for you?" The answer might then be: "If I
couldn't have the plans fast enough, then I
would run out of time, and I wouldn't
have continuity."

3. Your third and final investigation deals
with the emotions involved in your
customer not getting what he or she wants.
Start with an open-ended question: "What
would that be like for you?" You might get
an answer like, "I'd hate it," or "It would
make me uncomfortable," or "It would put
me way behind in my work."

If your customer does not respond to an
open-ended question, and no emotional
response is forthcoming, you might try a
closed-ended question: "Would that be

frustrating for you?," "Would that make you
angry?," "Would that put you at risk with
your boss?" or "Would that be scary?"

Now you know what's important to your
internal customer; you know the
consequences for them if they do not get
what is important to them; and, even more
powerfully, what emotions this would bring
up. This emotional situation is precisely
what you are going to go upstream to
head off.

EVALUATING YOUR PERFORMANCE.

Once you have done your investigation, the
next step is to deal with your *performance*
on the issues. This is one step that might be
uncomfortable for you. But doing it will
save you a tremendous amount of pain later
on. This step is to simply take the important
issues (important to your internal customer)
and do a fearless audit of how well you
perform on these issues.

For example, you may be very good at manipulating data on a computer, but you may be just terrible at keeping track of sheets of paper. You may be excellent at keeping track of the minutest detail, and just terrible at returning phone calls.

Whatever it is you are good at, or not good at, is extremely important for your internal customer to know about, so you can influence her or his expectations. Let's say you are very good at manipulating data, but you hate to return phone calls. And let's say, returning phone calls is the most important issue to your internal customer. If you do nothing about this, you are going to lose in an emotionally-charged situation. All of the problems will get magnified. Your not having returned phone calls and the consequences (the customer's emotions of anger and frustration) will all come up in your face.

However, if you make a commitment to improve your process of returning phone calls, you can head off a tremendous amount of grief. Right now you might be saying to yourself: "Why would I have to change? I hate to return phone calls and I'm not going to change just for this."

The good news is, you don't have to change yourself.

SYSTEM FAILURES.

What we are looking at here is your process. As stated before, Edwards Deming, the man who taught the Japanese how to manufacture using the most efficient, quality-focused techniques, says that "94% of failures are not people failures. They are system, or process failures." That means, if you do not return phone calls, it's simply a process failure. By looking at this task as a process, it opens up many alternatives you did not have before.

For example, when you get a phone call from a person, and you don't feel like returning it, simply hand it over to a co-worker you have enlisted to return the phone calls for you. (A co-worker who loves to talk on the phone.) Have that person return the phone calls promptly, and find out what needs to be done.

What you can do for the co-worker in return is to find out what that person hates to do that you may like, and make a trade out of it. As human beings, we all have things that we are good at and we love to do, and things we are not good at and we don't like to do. Fortunately, in any given situation, there is usually someone who can pick up the slack for you, and vice versa. That's how you can support each other. So, now you have improved some of the processes you are not good at.

HOW TO MANAGE EXPECTATIONS.

Now that you have lowered expectations in the area you don't do well, it's time to raise expectations in the parts you do well. For example, let's say one of the issues important to your customer is "altering plans quickly," and you are very, very good at that. At the same time, you are saying

you are not good at something (like
returning phone calls), say what you *are*
good at (altering plans quickly.)

You might say: "I can give you prompt
answers, as long as you can put up with
someone else returning your phone calls, or
my handling that in a different way." In
summary, if you do the following, you are
going to get great value out of this:

1. Raise their expectations on the important
issues on which you perform well.
2. Lower expectations on the important
issues on which you don't perform well.
These issues may be important enough for
them to take some action on their own. For
example, they can forgive you for not
returning phone calls promptly, they can
come to your office rather than calling, they
can work with someone else or they can not
call much.

What you have now is *negotiation* that will
prevent a lot of the problems from
occurring. Most problems are a function of
expectations. If you do not go through this

process, your internal customer will expect you to be good at all of the things that are important. Worse yet, you won't even know what the important things are, and, of course, you won't be good at all of them. So, you are set up for failure.

On the other hand, with your new process you have met, you have discussed the issues, negotiated and now you are expected to perform chiefly on the things you are good at. And, working together, you will get support with the things you are not good at.

Now that you have set up the expectations correctly, you can do the work in a much less emotionally-charged way. You are going into the work knowing exactly what is expected of you, and possibly without the feeling of the axe beginning to drop. The next step is to take your internal customer's issues and use those as a work priority plan.

SETTING UP A PRIORITY PLAN.

This plan concerns the most important aspects of the work that you are going to be

doing. It's a checkpoint against how well
you will know you are doing your work.

So do the work as you normally would,
making sure you perform well on the
important issues, and simply leave alone, or
don't focus too much on, the issues that are
unimportant. Now that the work is done, it's
time to present it to your internal customer.

MAKING AN EFFECTIVE PRESENTATION.

When you go back to your internal
customer, the place to start is not to show
him or her the work, but again revisit the
issues. (See "building the bridge" in chapter
20) "You said this is an important issue to
you, and that issue is important to you. And,
I said I am good at this issue and that issue,
and we negotiated another way to work on
issue number 3 that I am not so good at."

Right after that, you reaffirm your
commitment to that internal customer's
important issues, so the customer knows

their issues are your issues, and you have
been looking out for their interests. This
should make your presentation go much
more smoothly because you have negotiated
the level of expectation in the process, and
you've improved the process so it prevents
these situations. This, then, will take care of
80% or more of the emotionally-charged
situations. Simply by preventing
emotionally-charged situations from arising,
you have solved them.

MANAGING EMOTIONS.

There is, however, the 20% of emotions that
may come up. And this will happen no
matter how much you plan. There may be
an issue important to your customer that
neither one of you touched on in your
investigative phase, but has now come up in
the process of doing the work. Or there may
be an outcome in your work that brings up a
whole new set of issues, or brings up a set
of emotions attached to these issues.

If these emotions come up, most people want to run and hide. And yet the way to win in these situations is to do precisely the opposite: take them on and be clear and direct about them.

Often an emotion will come up and pervade a room, and yet no one will say anything about it. This means the emotion will be allowed to stay and grow. The best way to make an emotion go away is to acknowledge and bring it to the foreground. Only then will it go away.

Let's say you have brought in some incorrect data, and time is growing short. You can see your internal customer is agitated about this. Instead of defending yourself, *do the opposite*.

First, acknowledge what happened and what the emotion is. "It looks like the data is incorrect, and we are running late, and I'll bet that really frustrates you." You have just offered your customer an invitation to vent his or her emotions. The emotions won't go away until they can talk about it.

This is also an opportunity for you to get rid of any emotions you have. "I'm feeling ashamed this is late. I know if we can just work it out, we can still get it done so it won't be too late."

The way to get an emotion out of the room is to acknowledge it, and talk about it. The next step is to make a commitment to work out the problem. Without the emotion, both of you will be able to see the problem more clearly. (One further tip: Leave the history behind you. Another way is to make sure your conversation from that point on is forward. Not "Who is going to get the blame for this?" but "What are we going to do from here?")

Once the emotions are out of the room, and the conversation is forward, you have an opportunity to make a new set of agreements which both of you can approach with renewed enthusiasm, rather than anger, shame and blame. Something to watch out for here is once you have made this new set of agreements, be doubly sure you keep your agreements. Otherwise, the emotions that were attached to the last meeting will certainly resurface, and be intensified. Also, because these issues have been so emotionally-charged, these should move right to the top of your issues list.

The seven steps to manage emotionally-charged situations:

1. Go upstream to prevent 80% of the emotions. First, do that by investigating needs, finding out what the consequences are for not getting the needs met, and, finally, by finding out what emotions would be involved if those needs are not met. Now you know what can happen when things don't go well, and you also have the tools to avoid it.

2. Share the issues list and make sure the internal customer rates each issue so you know exactly what the important issues are.

3. Be brutally honest about your ability to perform on each issue. Tell them what you are good at and raise expectations. Also tell

them what you are not good at and lower
expectations. Then negotiate these issues so
you can get the support you need to perform
better on the important issues you do not do
well. Also, use the unimportant issues as a
source of funding for the time to do your
work. Do just enough to maintain your
performance on these unimportant issues, or
when it's safe, leave them alone.

4. Begin working, using the issues as your
work priority plan. Do the work as you
normally would, and then present the work.

5. When presenting your work, use the
issues as the context for presenting your
work, and reaffirm the commitment to your
internal customer's important issues. This
will take care of 80% of the emotional
situations.

6. When new emotionally-charged
situations come up (the other 20%,) first
deal with the emotions. Acknowledge them
verbally, both the customer's and yours. It's
the only way to make them go away. Next,
make sure the conversation is moving

forward, rather than dwelling on the history of what happened. This will get you out of blame, shame, justification and defense, and into a new set of agreements.

7. Finally, keep those new set of agreements as though your life depended on it. Because of the emotional charge you have seen, this will be the most important set of agreements you make. If you follow these steps, you will be able to deal with emotionally charged situations, without suffering from the emotions. And, in fact, you will even have an opportunity to perform brilliantly in a job you thought you may not be able to perform in at all.

Quick Reference Guide
THIS IS THE WHOLE BOOK IN TWO MINUTES. IT'S THAT SIMPLE.

"Stop looking for what seems to be missing. You have everything you need to start with – nothing."
    – Author Unknown

Innovate with C.A.R.E.

WHAT: The four innovation types. Creator, Advancer, Refiner, Executor.
WHY: So people can be in their right place and understand each other.
WHEN: About 3 minutes reading time.
WHERE: Chapter 2, Pages 11-18.

How to work with Creators.

WHAT: Give a Creator recognition, authenticity, respect and distinctiveness to break down traditional barriers.
WHY: You'll have an inspired innovation ally that can give you your best opportunities.
WHEN: About 4 minutes reading time.
WHERE: Chapter 4, Pages 29-35.

How to be a Creator.

WHAT: There is but one unifying principle in all powerful creativity. Opposites.

You can use this powerful principle in a simple four-step method to solve all kinds of problems. Even those you think you can't.

1. OUTCOME. Decide what you want to accomplish.

2. OBVIOUS. Determine the strongest beliefs you have about each part of the outcome.

3. OPPOSITE. Create a statement contradicting these beliefs.

4. "OPPOTUNITY." (A unity of opposites that cause an opportunity.)

Stretch your mind to come up with an idea you've never thought before.

The more extreme the opposites, the more powerful the effect. (In a film the director plays a brutal murder scene to happy music. A father instantly arouses his hard-to-wake child by telling her it's time to go to sleep.)

To get the most extreme new belief or idea (the opposite,) increase your distance with the most extreme old belief (the obvious.)

Example: You've heard the old saying: "He's such a good salesman, he can sell refrigerators to Eskimos."

1. OUTCOME. Start with a "do what to whom" statement (the outcome).

Example: Sell refrigerators to Eskimos.

2. OBVIOUS. Find the obvious beliefs about that statement the "word association" game: Sky-blue, stove-hot, dog-cat. (The first word that pops into your mind when you say another word). Make the association into a sentence: "The sky is blue." "A stove is hot." "A dog chases cats."

Example: Refrigerators keep things cool.
Eskimos live in the North.

3. OPPOSITE. Then, in the context of the
old belief, insert the opposite to create a
contradiction.

Example: Refrigerators keep things warm.
Eskimos live in the South.

4. "OPPOTUNITY." Lastly, look at your
contradictory statement and ask "How could
this be true?"

Example: A refrigerator can keep things
warm in extreme cold because its insulation
keeps food from freezing.
Eskimos can live in the South simply by
moving. (To Phoenix, or anywhere else.)
Then you can sell them a refrigerator: (For
their condo instead of their igloo.)

PLACES TO LOOK.

1. Domain: Content/Context. The power is
in changing the context, look at the bigger

picture. Ghandi changed the context of war and won by not fighting.

2. Focus: Person/Product. Focus on the person, not what you're trying to sell. It's been said that "selling is 1/4 inch drills and marketing is 1/4 inch holes."

3. Development: Sophisticated/Simple. Find the simplicity that comes after the sophistication. *"For simplicity on this side of complexity, I would not give a whit. For simplicity on the other side of complexity, I would give my life."*
  –Oliver Wendell Holmes

4. Physical: Tangible/Intangible. Use tangibles to sell intangibles (Prudential's Rock) and intangibles to sell intangibles. (Coke's "Real Thing.")

5. Visual: Unity/Contrast. Look for similar shapes, colors or other physical realities. Then, be sure the two elements that look alike are as opposite in meaning as possible. (A Scotch Brand Tape dispenser and a snail.)

6. Verbal: Figurative/Literal. Many literal meanings become figurative over time. The opportunity is to juxtapose them with an opposite literal meaning. (Drug poster, showing stupid user: "Why do you think they call it "dope?")

7. Quantity: Single/Multiple. Just because numbers seem real, we expect them to be a certain way. Sadaharu Oh, the Japanese Home Run King (more than 800 career homers), stood on one leg, not two, when he batted.

THE NINE DOTS.

Every creativity book features the nine dots, the exercise that teaches you to think outside boundaries of your own limitations. If you don't recall, you must connect all nine dots, covering each of them at least once.
The pencil cannot leave the surface while drawing the solution.

The problem with that exercise: It doesn't give you a specific place outside the nine dots to go. So when it comes to actually solving the problem, you're still left on your own (albeit in a place where you do have a chance.)

That's why we will now apply the power and focus of opposites to this familiar problem.

When solving physical problems start by considering the four domains of physical reality: Space, time, energy and matter. For reference I have supplied two sets of commonly used opposites for each. Choose the most obvious word in each set, then ask yourself how its opposite could be true.

The Nine Dots, Solution 1: Space, In/Out. This is the most common solution, achieved by moving outside the mythical square.

Solution 2: Space, Here/There. To cover all the dots in ONE straight line, simply circle the earth twice catching three dots with each pass.

Solution 3: Time, Now/Then. Since the problem is "now," go back to the past when the number base was two. Then, you would count to four straight lines like this: 1, 10, 11, 100. You now have 100 straight lines to cover the dots.

Solution 4: Time, Fast/Slow. Since this is a relatively "slow" process, go to the opposite, "fast." Now, you're restricted by how you move the pencil, but not the paper. Shake the paper across the pencil as fast as you can. See how you cover the dots.

Solution 5: Matter, Tangible/Intangible. It's a tangible puzzle, so use an intangible solution, trust. Hide the paper and say "Trust that I solved it."

Solution 6: Matter, Big/Small. You're using a small pencil. Get a big one, bigger than all the dots. Cover them all in one pass. Or expand the dots so they're so big they merge into one big dot. Now cover it in one pass.

Solution 7: Energy, Hot/Cold. The paper is colder than your body temperature. So, go to the opposite, "hot." Set the paper on fire (in a safe place) and wait until it curls into a small ash. Cover all nine dots in one pass on the ash.

Solution 8: Energy, Positive/Negative. The paper is white, a positive color. Color it black, a negative color. The black dots will blend into the paper. Now, get anyone to prove that you didn't cover the dots in one pass. Try and find the dots.

YOU'VE JUST FINISHED THE TWO-MINUTE VERSION OF INNOVATION ON DEMAND.

There. That's it. That's all you need to know. Now try it. Apply Innovation on Demand to anything that will produce value for you.

Here's the method for you to refer to when you need it.

1. OUTCOME. Start with a "do what to whom" statement (the outcome.)

2. OBVIOUS. Find the obvious beliefs about that statement with the "word association" game: Sky-blue, stove-hot, dog-cat. Make the association into a sentence: "The sky is blue." "A stove is hot." "A dog chases cats."

3. OPPOSITE. Then, in the context of the old belief, insert the opposite to create a contradiction.

4. "OPPOTUNITY." Lastly, look at your contradictory statement and ask "How could this be true?" The answer to this question may hold a great "oppotunity" for you.

WHY: To create the powerful innovation and change that is needed in '90's and beyond.
WHEN: About 6 minutes reading time.
WHERE: Chapters 5-14, Pages 37-166.

How to structure an innovation team for best results.

WHAT: **1**. Objectives and scope.
(Leader: Department Head, V.P. or C.E.O.)
2. Create team Selection Criteria.
(Leader: Department Head, V.P. or C.E.O.)
3. Select team. (Leader: Department Head, V.P. or C.E.O.)
4. Align team. (Leader: Facilitator)

5. Develop strategy. (Leader: Refiner)
6. Create concept. (Leader: Creator)
7. Test concept. (Leader: Advancer)
8. Plan implementation. (Leader: Refiner)
9. Implement. (Leader: Executor)
WHY: So people can work together for best results.
WHEN: About 4 minutes reading time.
WHERE: Chapter 3, Pages 19-26.

How to get the most useful information.

WHAT: The importance-performance issues grid.
WHY: Focus on the customers most important criteria for your success.
WHEN: About 12 minutes reading time.
WHERE: Chapter 19, Pages 195-216.

How to stand out from the competition.

WHAT: OppoScales. Find out which way your competitor is leaning.
WHY: So you can stand in the opposite place and push hard for maximum leverage.
WHEN: About 2 minutes reading time.
WHERE: Chapter 19, Pages 195-216.

How to get unstuck.

WHAT: The most common places Creators
get stuck creating.
OUTCOME. Not knowing what you want.
OUTCOME. Choosing an outcome that's no
different from what you have.
OBVIOUS. Using word associations that
aren't obvious enough.
OBVIOUS. Forgetting to put the obvious
words into a sentence context.
OPPOSITE. Thinking that words have only
one opposite.
OPPOSITE. Failing to recognize shades
of meaning.
"OPPOTUNITY." Stopping at only one
solution.
"OPPOTUNITY." Failing to document your
results, then forgetting. Write them down.
PERFECT, YET, STILL NO RESULTS. Do
the opposite of the method, and find
something even more powerful.
WHY: Solve the 20 per cent of the problems
that create 80 per cent of the frustration.
WHEN: About 4 minutes reading time.
WHERE: Chapter 21, Pages 227-234.

How to choose the best ideas.

WHAT: The four "U's" of element combining. Ubiquity, Uniquity, Unity and Utility.
WHY: Criteria for selecting the best idea for the need. Balancing power with practicality.
WHEN: About 2 minutes reading time.
WHERE: Chapter 18, Pages 191-193.

How to test ideas.

WHAT: Avoid the two most common errors in powerful ideas; going over the line in clarity and taste.
WHY: So you can be congruent with your audience's perceptions.
WHEN: About 2 minutes reading time.
WHERE: Chapter 17, Pages 185-189.

How to sell even the most innovative ideas.

WHAT: **1.** Go opposite the conventional selling wisdom and win.
2. Go in the opposite direction and build the bridge from their side of the river.

WHY: So people can get through their own habits and see things your way.

WHEN: About 4 minutes reading time.

WHERE: Chapter 20, Pages 217-225.

How to manage expectations for success.

WHAT: Raise expectations on issues where you perform well (issues grid,) lower expectations on issues where you don't perform well.

WHY: If you keep expectations within range, you'll always succeed.

WHEN: About 6 minutes reading time.

WHERE: Qualitivity, Pages 237-260.

The Oxymoron Hall of Fame
HAVE SOME FUN WITH OPPOSITES.

From *Jumbo Shrimp and other Oxymorons*, Blumenfield, (Putnam) and other street sources.

OXYMORONIC LOGIC
BLAMELESS CULPRITS
UNSUNG HEROES
TREMENDOUSLY SMALL
PERMANENTLY TEMPORARY
REAL POTENTIAL
POLITICAL PROMISE
ESSENTIALLY AGREE
OBSCURELY OBVIOUS
SPECIAL-BUT IN THE SAME WAY
IMPORTANT TRIVIA
DEFINITELY PROBABLY
AND/OR
OLD AGE
INITIAL CONCLUSION
PLANNED SERENDIPITY
MISCELLANEOUS AND/OR OTHER
WORKING VACATIONS
BACK-UP FORWARD

FAST FOOD
ACADEMIC SALARY
NEW, IMPROVED
FEDERAL ASSISTANCE
CONSTANT VARIABLE
LIGHT OPERA
TALL JOCKEY
SECOND DEADLINE
FULL PROFESSOR
SLIGHTLY PREOCCUPIED
JUMBO SHRIMP
FREEZER BURN
EVEN ODDS
DIVORCE COURT
NEAR MISS
CARDINAL SIN
GOOD LOSER
SLIGHTLY PREGNANT
AMTRAK SCHEDULE
CIVIL WAR
CLEAN DIRT
CRIMINAL JUSTICE
ALMOST SUDDENLY
STANDARD DEVIATIONS
LOVE-HATE
MANIC DEPRESSIVE
TALK SHOWS
LIVE TELEVISION

GOOD NEWS
RESOLUTE AMBIVALENCE
LOCAL NETWORK
ARROGANT HUMILITY
THREE ORIGINALS
ORIGINAL COPY
MILITARY INTELLIGENCE
AIRLINE FOOD
SEMI PERFECT
IDIOT SAVANT
DELIBERATE SPEED
INTENSE APATHY
MILD INTEREST
PARTIAL SUCCESS
FIRST ANNUAL
SOUND JUDGEMENT
EXTENSIVE BRIEFING
CHAOTIC ORGANIZATION
BITTERSWEET
SWEET AND SOUR
LEGAL BRIEF
TEXAS CHIC
FACULTY COOPERATION
SOPHISTICATED NEW YORKER
FORM LETTERS
CONSTRUCTIVE CRITICISM
ONLY CHOICE
PARTIAL SENSE
OLD NEWS
HOME OFFICE

GENUINE IMITATION
BAD SEX
JUSTIFIABLE HOMICIDE
CONVENTIONAL WISDOM
KICKSTAND
CLOSED WINDOW
VACUUM PACKED
CASUAL SEX
GLOBAL VILLAGE
NORMAL HUMAN
TRUE ILLUSION
WHITE GOLD
EXACT ESTIMATE
LIMITED OBLIGATION
ABUNDANT POVERTY
TRAFFIC FLOW
RUSH HOUR
CAB DRIVER
STATE OWNERSHIP
CASUALLY ELEGANT
FISH FARM
MINOR MIRACLE
FAMILY LIFE
DISTANT RELATIVES
FAMILY LIFE
HOME COOKING
REAL MAGIC
ELECTED KING

FAIRLY STABLE
GEORGIA PEACHES (come from South Carolina)
SERIOUS HUMOR
ROLLING STOP
NATIONAL LOCAL
OFFICE WORK
BUSINESS SCHOOL
FRIENDLY TAKEOVER
CORPORATE PLANNING
FINAL ROUGH
PLANNED CHANGE
DEATH BENEFITS
NEGATIVE INCOME
BANKER'S TRUST
ZERO DEFECTS
OFFICE SPACE
ACCURATELY REPORTED
MY OWN BUSINESS
CLASSIC NEW MOVIES
METAL WOOD
FALCON DEFENSE
YOGI BERRA LANGUAGE
BRAVES FANS
FEMALE JOCK
MINNESOTA BASKETBALL
FOOTBALL GAME
PASSIVE AGGRESSIVE
SCHOOL VACATION

JOB SATISFACTION
LESSER EVIL
AUTOMOTIVE SCIENCE
SPEED WALKING
FRESH RAISINS
NON-DAIRY CREAMER
WHITE ROSE
BAKED ALASKA
LASTING FAD
WHITE BURGUNDY
FROZEN FOOD
EDUCATED GUESS
EXPRESS MAIL
WELL-KEPT SECRET
IOWA CITY
DOWNTOWN LOS ANGELES
SMALLER HALF
TRUTH IN ADVERTISING
MODERN HISTORY
PURE .999 SILVER
PUBLIC SERVICE
TAPED LIVE
LIMITED NUCLEAR WAR
WAR GAMES
SOCIAL SECURITY
FAIRLY CERTAIN
COLLEGE MEN
FEMALE MAILMEN

JUNIOR OFFICERS
SENIOR ACCOUNT EXEC
POSTAL SERVICE
FEDERAL BUDGET
CIVIL SERVICE
UNITED NATIONS
TAX RETURN
LEGAL LANGUAGE
FINAL REVISION
POLITICAL PROMISE
UNWRITTEN LAW
SPARE TIME
SCIENCE FICTION
PARTLY SUNNY
WEATHER FORECAST
SUN SHOWERS
SOFT ROCK
ROCK MUSIC
BOY GEORGE
GUEST HOST
EDUCATIONAL TELEVISION
INSTANT REPLAY
GOOD GRIEF
SILENT SCREAM
CRIMINAL LAWYER
MILITARY ADVISER
BABY DOCTOR
PAINLESS DENTIST
COMMERCIAL ARTIST

Bibliography
WHERE TO READ FURTHER.

Burgess, Anthony, *A Clockwork Orange*, (W.W. Norton, 1963.)

Carlzon, Jan, *Moments Of Truth*, Ballinger (Publications Co., 1987.)

DeBono, Edward, *Lateral Thinking*, (Harper and Row, 1970.)

Della Femina, Jerry , *From Those Wonderful Folks Who Gave You Pearl Harbor*, (Simon and Schuster, 1970.)

Land, George Ainsworth, *Grow Or Die*, (Wiley, 1986.)

Ogilvy, David, *Confessions Of An Advertising Man*, (Atheneum Press, 1963.)

Osborn, Alexander, *Applied Imagination*, (Scribner, 1953.)

Patent, Arnold, *You Can Have It All: The Art Of Winning*, (Money Mastery Publs., 1984.)

Peters, Thomas J., *Thriving On Chaos*,
(Knopf, 1987. Distributor: Random House.)

Rakham, Neil, *S.P.I.N. Selling*, (McGraw-Hill, 1988.)

Sculley, John, *Odyssey: Pepsi To Apple*,
(Harper and Row, 1987.)

Thrift, Syd, *The Game According To Syd*,
(Simon and Schuster, 1990.)

Toffler, Alvin, *Future Shock*, (Random House, 1970.)

Toffler, Alvin, *Power Shift*, (Bantam Books, 1990.)

Walton, Mary, *Deming Management Method*, (Dodd-Mead, 1986.)

Wilson, Larry & Johnson, Spencer,
The One-Minute Sales Person, (W. Morrow, 1984.)

INNOVATE WITH C.A.R.E. is a registered trademark of Carlson Learning Company. (Used with permission.)